JJ's JOURNEY

JJ's JOURNEY

A Story of Heroes and Heart

Tracy Calhoun & JJ

DIVERSIONBOOKS

Diversion Books
A Division of Diversion Publishing Corp.
443 Park Avenue South, Suite 1008
New York, New York 10016
www.DiversionBooks.com

For more information, email info@diversionbooks.com

First Diversion Books edition October 2017.
Hardcover ISBN: 978-1-63576-044-6
eBook ISBN: 978-1-63576-043-9

Printed in the U.S.A.
SDB/1708
1 3 5 7 9 10 8 6 4 2

To my husband, Tellus,
for helping to turn a Montana girl into the Crazy Dog Lady

1

I have always heard people mention something going "viral" online, but never knew what that really meant—certainly not from personal experience. I started a Facebook page separate from my personal profile the year the Hospice House opened to share stories of the power of the human-animal bond. At the time, I was only a user of Facebook, and had not yet explored the other social media platforms, so I wanted to stay with something familiar. I thought a separate page would allow me to have a place where I could keep tales related to my therapy dog work. In the first year, I had about 200 followers, mostly friends and family, with a few family members of former hospice patients. I shared photos and articles about therapy dogs, including sagas featuring my Golden Retriever, JJ.

Long before I started work at Samaritan Evergreen Hospice, the director's dream for the program included opening an inpatient hospice facility, where patients could be admitted when they needed more intense symptom management. It was years in the making and the effort was largely driven by our local community because they saw the benefit in having such a special place. As it turns out, residents and businesses made donations not only to buy the land, but to build and furnish the Hospice House in its entirety.

By the time these dreams were coming to fruition, I had been working as an outpatient hospice nurse with Samaritan for several years. Long before working at Samaritan, I started my hospice career at an inpatient hospice facility in Washington State. Since I was the only person on staff who had ever worked at an inpatient hospice facility, I had been invited to help with the details of the construction. JJ was just over a year old at the time, and she made many trips through the building before we accepted our first patient.

JJ has been a fixture at our inpatient hospice from opening day, and I consider it a gift to have her at work with me. Because of her popularity with patients and family members, I decided to let her sassy and spirited voice speak on what evolved into her Facebook page by presenting most of the posts through JJ's eyes. From the early days online, I shared not only about JJ's visits with those who were dying, but with all who met her at the Hospice House. Occasionally, I took photos to help to tell her story. There have even been a couple of rare instances when JJ's interactions have been caught on video. I had originally posted one of these videos on her Facebook page less than two years after we opened the Hospice House. By that time, we had more followers, but it was still a small number of people, totaling less than seven hundred. Many of these included family members who continued to follow her after their loved ones died, some sharing photos and stories along the way. While remembering the death of a family member can be hard, reconnecting with a fun-loving and tender-hearted dog has been a highlight for many and continues to this day. For several, she was and continues to be a bright light during a very sad time.

My primary role is as a therapy dog at our Hospice House in Oregon. You can think of me as a part-time residential dog, since I work twelve-hour shifts with The One In Charge (aka The Bossy One, TBO, BossyPants, CrankyPants, whatever the mood). She is a hospice nurse and my driver. We have a busy life, but I am the queen of self-care and spend a lot of time just having fun. On occasion, I am even a nanny to puppies. At work, I help support staff, volunteers,

patients, families, and visitors. Often, I'm just a silly distraction and am good at insisting on a belly rub. Sometimes, I make the best one to support grieving loved ones, because words often are inadequate, but a dog's unconditional love provides so much. I have been in this role since we opened our inpatient hospice facility and have been an official therapy dog since I turned one and passed my test (barely). We have many staff, families, and volunteers who follow my story, so it's nice to balance the tough, heart-wrenching stuff with light-hearted moments and play. I'm told if humans led a life balanced like this, they would do well. Personally, I think bacon helps, A LOT!

The video I posted shows JJ up on the bed with a woman I will call Grace. Grace was in her nineties, was blind, and had never married, so she had no family members. She did have some very devoted caregivers, who had been doing their best to help this very headstrong, independent elderly woman live alone at home. Grace was incredibly frail and had some bruises on her arms, which wasn't surprising to us when we learned she'd had a big fall that sent her to the hospital. Grace's nails were nicely manicured, thanks to the attention of one of our CNAs several hours earlier. We had noticed old, chipped polish on her nails, so a fresh manicure was done to show her dignity, even if she was not aware of it. By the time she arrived at the Hospice House, Grace had no purposeful movement, something very common for people who are getting close to death. We learned she was fond of audiobooks, specifically poetry. The day I took the video, we had a reading of Yeats playing in the background. In hospice, we frequently tell family members that we believe people can still hear us toward the end of their lives, even if they are not able to acknowledge us the way they normally would. On this day, it was quiet toward the end of my shift, so I decided to sit at Grace's bedside so she wasn't alone. It is common for JJ to accompany me at times like this and she did that evening. I had been told Grace was fond of dogs, so when JJ indicated she would like to get up onto the bed, I carefully placed her next to Grace and then settled into my chair. JJ often will nudge her muzzle under someone's hand, even if they are not responding. I'm not sure how I thought to record this very private, intimate moment, but something about it was just incredibly touching to witness and I wanted to remember it. While I only got a couple of minutes on video, it was striking to watch JJ nudge these very thin fingers until, after a while, those fingers moved a bit in response marking Grace's first deliberate movement of the day, possibly her last deliberate movement ever. On the video, it even looked like Grace poked JJ's eye at one point, though from my vantage point JJ had her eyes tightly shut and wasn't poked or bothered by it. Shortly after this, JJ fell asleep with Grace's hand resting on her head. They stayed this way for close to twenty minutes, while I just sat at the bedside. JJ has been known to fall asleep during a bed visit, but only if I stayed nearby. At other times, she has only stayed briefly before deciding to get off the bed. She clearly was very comfortable where she was. When we came back to work the next day, I found out Grace had died peacefully early in the morning, and I was thankful for our time together the day before.

Later, when I watched the video, I saw that I didn't capture any identifying information, which enabled me to share it without concerns of violating Grace's privacy. The few people who saw the video were very moved by it, as I had been.

Our days continued as usual, playing hard during our off time and going about our hospice care as we always had. JJ worked to perfect her mooching skills, and I was still sharing her antics and heartwarming moments with others online.

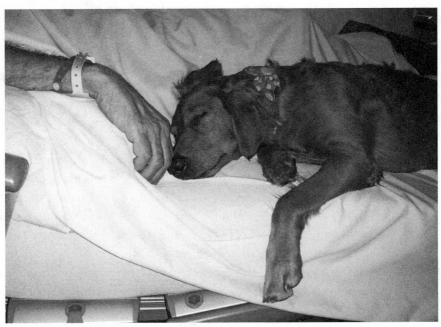

BossyPants and I only worked a half-day today, and we happened to have visited someone getting close to his time to say goodbye. On these quiet days, we are able to spend time sitting with people who are alone, and sometimes I do a bed visit, like I did today. We had our music therapist's harp CD playing in the background, as it can help soothe and slow down the respiratory pattern of a person who is having difficulty breathing. There are many options used to help comfort people at times like this, including me. This gentleman loved dogs and loved talking to me when he was able. It might look like all I did was sleep on the job today, but it was good work I did for his family. I was honored to have been "his" dog for the day.

One day, nearly two years later, someone online asked me what I meant by "bed visit," so I re-shared the video I had posted of JJ and Grace. We were in the middle of working six out of seven days, our long monthly stretch. When I checked my phone on breaks, I noticed a puzzling jump in social media activity. Somehow, the video had gone viral in the two days since I re-shared it. Then, I received an e-mail request for a phone interview with *King 5 News* in Seattle at work. As a nurse, I am not used to having someone want to interview me, and I felt as though I stammered through my answers, still in disbelief that a news media organization wanted to hear the story behind my short video. Once the interview aired, I had many requests from others. During my day off I did interviews with *Huffington Post*, *The Dodo*, *Three Million Dogs*, and *Fox 13* in Tampa. The following day there continued to be interest from various media outlets. *USA Today*, *ABC World News Tonight*, *BuzzFeed Español*, and *Inside Edition* all wanted to speak to me while I was at work. My supervisor called in another nurse to relieve me just so I could answer JJ's media requests. It happened to be a day when we had fewer patients, so we had a nurse on call that could easily cover my work. My supervisors and the hospice staff were all quite excited by the attention, and were very supportive of me taking time to field phone calls. They also had been keeping track of the sudden popularity of JJ's page and kept asking me: "how many followers now?" After a while, it was difficult to respond to the interview questions over and over without the answers sounding canned to my ears. At the same time, I was deluged by messages from curious viewers asking how to make their dog a therapy dog, requesting a visit for an ill relative (who was often overseas), and how to get involved with my organization.

E-mails and messages continued to roll in throughout the coming days, including from friends and family who reported seeing news about us. Apparently, a brief mention of the video ran on many local news stations across the country and was on the *Today Show* as well. It was fun to hear from a family member of one of our previous patients, who said: "We saw you on the local news down here in Atlanta. It's so awesome! My grandmother was in your hospice last year in September and I always remember JJ, and having to share my french fries with her. It's such an awesome thing you guys do. I am so proud that my grandmother was so well taken care of while she was there."

I got a text from my cousin showing me JJ's photo in an article in the August 26 edition of *USA Today*. After work, as my husband and I were headed to find a copy, I got a phone call from our on-call nurse, who handles all the calls for our home hospice patients after hours. "Someone from *NBC* is looking for you." *What?* By the end of the week, the story was featured across a wide variety of online media outlets around the world. A few of these international outlets included *The Daily News* and *The Mirror* in London, *The New Indian Express* in Delhi, as well as *Good Morning America, AOL, The Examiner, I Heart Dogs, BarkPost,* and *People Pets Magazine.* I think the most interesting one I saw was featured on the *Daily Braille.* It was incredibly appropriate to have an article written in Braille that described the interaction between JJ and a dying woman who was blind. To this day, I have never been able to go back far enough to figure out who shared the video and started the viral madness. It became clear that the story was shared widely across the world, touching people in areas where they don't even have hospice.

Along the way, I did my best to try to keep up with the messages and comments that were piling up, but I gave up when the video's comments reached 15,000. For the most part, the responses I saw were positive and memorable. Within one week, because of the video, JJ's page went from reaching approximately 5,000 people to over 27 million. I was not amazed at the response people had after watching this powerful example of the human-animal connection, but I was stunned by how far and how many it reached. It was clear people around the world were touched by their brief glimpse into the innate qualities of JJ that made her such a great therapy dog. Since I share my life with her, I get to see how much more there is to this loving, tender, generous, goofy, and fun-loving dog.

2

When people meet JJ, one of the most common questions I get asked is how I got started with therapy dogs. As a child growing up in Montana, we had dogs, cats, horses, and even parakeets, so it's not a surprise I would have animals around me as an adult. In high school, when considering college options with my guidance counselor, I struggled for awhile trying to decide what career might interest me. As much as I loved animals, veterinary medicine never crossed my mind.

When looking through information from all the different colleges, I read about nursing school and was drawn to the idea of combining science with helping others. I had no one around me or in my family that was in nursing, other than an aunt who lived in Minnesota. I had never even considered it until I read about nursing schools in the different brochures. From that day forth, I knew I would be a nurse. It has turned out to be one of the best decisions I have ever made and my nursing career has been an excellent fit for my life. Approximately half of our graduating class of 99 students considered leaving the state to pursue post-high school options, including myself. I headed to Washington State and graduated four years later with my Bachelor of Science in Nursing from Pacific Lutheran University, class of 1988. I loved the combination of mountains and water in Washington State, and decided to stay in the greater Seattle area after graduation.

Six years later, I was working as a hospice nurse at an inpatient hospice facility in Washington State. I was familiar with the use of animals in therapeutic contexts, but was inspired by a local news story about volunteering with therapy dogs and thought it might be a good job for my first Golden Retriever, Booker. We took some classes, found it was a good fit, and went on to become a registered therapy dog team. We started volunteering at a transitional housing unit for mothers and their children after they had been at a shelter. We would visit weekly in the evening when the Moms would have their support group and the kids were all gathered together in a separate area. The kids ranged from young toddlers to young teenagers, but Booker was a calm Golden, who loved to be petted by anyone. He won everyone over, even those who had not been exposed to dogs and were timid in the beginning. Booker was helpful in defusing any conflict within the group, and he had many confidential conversations with kids during our visits. When someone needed to talk to him, I would retreat to the end of my leash and turn my back, to give them privacy. It was common to peek over my shoulder and witness them both lying on the ground, face-to-face, engaging in a full-fledged whispery conversation. It turns out dogs are excellent listeners, often much better than people, especially for these kids. Booker also was a great motivator, encouraging them to do things they were reluctant to do. The simple reward of being the one who got to throw a ball for him once a certain task was completed was often all the incentive they needed.

Our weekly visits became the highlight not only for the kids, but for their mothers as well. We got used to spending a little extra time at the end to let the moms say hi to Booker when they collected their kids. It didn't take long for me to recognize the value therapy dogs bring when interacting with people during sad or stressful times.

After volunteering with Booker, I started thinking about other settings where therapy dogs could be used. Knowing how stressful end of life care is for all involved, I thought our inpatient hospice would be a perfect place to have therapy dogs visit. It was the mid-90s, and therapy dogs were still quite a novelty in many healthcare settings. However, I was aware of the pet therapy dog program at the Children's Hospital in Denver, Colorado. They had been having dogs visit the hospital since 1984, so there clearly was precedent. We had a group of local therapy dog handlers express interest in visiting the hospice center with their dogs, but at the time there was no policy in place for this. I decided to get involved to advocate for starting a therapy dog program at our facility. Despite explaining how the relationship worked and telling the touching stories of the therapy dog interactions I was having with Booker, I ran up against a fair amount of resistance. It was still a unique idea in 1995, and there were many questions that needed answered, including: how teams would be selected, what kind of visiting times would be acceptable, what would the process be for visiting, and would the handlers need to go through the regular hospice volunteer training. I remained persistent and helped to get those questions answered over time.

She helped get a therapy dog program going at the inpatient hospice she worked at during a time when it wasn't very accepted. She's been a BossyPants forever and is remembered for it there.

A few years ago, I was corresponding with someone in relation to therapy dogs. I had no idea there would be any kind of connection to my former workplace, but after e-mailing back and forth for a bit, this woman finally figured out who I was. Apparently, in my determination to get a therapy dog program started, I unknowingly became a bit of a legend. I had no idea stories were told about "the nurse named Tracy" who made such impact on hospice, convincing those in charge that animals should be included. I still laugh when I think about this. As nurses, we can all be quite persistent, and at times, a bit obnoxious when it comes to advocating for our people. I'm quite certain others involved during that time could provide more interesting adjectives. Bossy, stubborn, and obstinate are just a few, though if I'm honest, my family, friends, and teachers all probably used these while I was growing up. When JJ and I were in Washington in 2014 for a HOPE Animal-Assisted Crisis Response deployment following the Oso landslide, I had the opportunity between callouts to drive down to the hospice center to say hello. So much had changed, and I was most proud to learn they had gained a large group of volunteer therapy dog teams that were making regular visits almost twenty years after I did my work as the persistent nurse advocate.

• • •

JJ is my fourth therapy dog partner. Many years after Booker, my dog Callie became a registered therapy dog. Callie was the second dog to work at our hospice program, joining Marfa, another nurse's dog, back in 2008. At that time, our hospice program only saw patients in their own homes or at facilities. Callie was JJ's nanny and early mentor. JJ's mother, Gamine, also became a therapy dog, completing her first therapy dog evaluation on the same day JJ did.

It is interesting how temperament moves through bloodlines. JJ got her calmness from her mama, but her sister Ottie is another story. Ottie was originally placed with a local family when she was a puppy and was mostly raised by their teenage son. We received a call when the son headed to college, asking if we would take her back. When Ottie returned to us, I had the idea of testing her for therapy work. Several of their siblings had passed their therapy dog tests and were making visits with their respective owners in various parts of the country. HA! It was like the circus came to town as we walked into the building and made an extremely brief jaunt around while she channeled the personality of her crazy father, Dash. I'm quite certain "calm" would not be an adjective used to describe the occasion. Rather, she brought her party shoes and I just hung my head, shaking it and laughing at the same time as we walked back to the car. Being a dog handler can certainly be humbling at times. It just goes to show not every dog has the personality to do the work JJ does, even with a lot of training and preparation.

When JJ was a puppy, I started by getting her out and exposed to as many diverse and novel situations and people as I could think of—though I am much better at doing this now than I was when JJ was young. Over the years, time and experience have added to my list of things to do with preparation for possible therapy dog work. Each dog I have worked with has taught me something new, and I learn more and more the longer I do therapy dog work.

Socialization is incredibly important for young puppies, but it is a concept that is often misunderstood. Many people think it means going to a puppy class, but socialization involves not only being introduced to other dogs, but also people (especially children), animals, environments, objects, among so many other things. We now know the critical time in a dog's life for socialization occurs between three and twelve to sixteen weeks, although it is important to continue to socialize older puppies and adult dogs through their lives. During this window of time, it is necessary to ensure that the puppy or dog has safe and positive interactions.

JJ started coming to our hospice office when she was three months old. There is no doubt how much people love interacting with a puppy, and this was no exception. She got to know every person who worked there and developed her mooching style very early on. I didn't know many people with young children, and I hadn't realized I was missing an important stage of training until confronted by it firsthand. In those days, our hospice director would bring her young granddaughter to work on occasion. Our old office building was a maze of hallways and small rooms. On this day, JJ was off the leash and checking in with different people. All of a sudden, I heard a big "woof-woof-woof." No one had ever heard her voice before so I went running. I found JJ completely perplexed by the apparition in front of her. A little person with long hair and a tutu was spinning around and around laughing hysterically at the silly puppy, while a children's movie (probably *The Little Mermaid*) played in the background. The silly and star-tled puppy seemed to be thinking, "what the heck is THIS?" As when any good training opportunity presents itself, we spent a fair amount of time with treats and the child, working on desensitizing JJ to this fascinating creature. After that, I started asking any parent on the street "can my puppy meet your child?" to continue her training. I now have a larger group of people from all makes, ages, and sizes to pool from when needing puppy socialization, so I no longer need to accost perfect strangers on the street. It's much less awkward that way, though it's certainly easy to find people who want to pet a puppy when out in public.

I was fortunate to have the permission of two local facilities, one an assisted living and the other a skilled nursing home, to make training visits with JJ when she was a puppy. These were facilities I had visited with Callie, and the staff recognized the value of training more therapy dogs and they were more than happy to help JJ's training. We made rounds, walking the halls and greeting people. There were plenty of walkers and wheelchairs to get exposed to, as well as the wonderful elevator with its noises and movements. Anyone who has met JJ would not be surprised to hear she was a food-motivated puppy. Treats were a great way to get her through anything that made her nervous. She looked forward to those elevator rides, as she considered them a magical doggie Pez dispenser. The assisted living facility was a more predictable environment with carpeting, many residents who could walk, and in general was a less noisy setting than the nursing home. We did many of our training visits there, but would do some visits at the skilled nursing facility as well. The linoleum, medical equipment, and larger number of busy staff made it a bit more challenging for a young dog, so I limited how often we trained there. I did as much as I could to get her prepared for our therapy dog test.

JJ was tested the day after she turned one and all went fairly well. The neutral dog test component however, was a bit dicey. We had to walk past another handler with a dog and greet them briefly without the dogs interacting. We did pass, although the evaluator and I both were aware that JJ was handicapped a bit simply by her youth and inexperience. The evaluator did say, "please bring her back to me for her re-test. I think she will really be a nice therapy dog as she grows up."

That same day, I also tested Gamine for the first time—at the ripe age of almost nine. I thought it would be good to have the option of having two therapy dogs available for volunteering. To no one's surprise, Gamine passed with flying colors, although we did have one little hiccup. One of the obedience elements of the test is to walk away from your dog to the end of the leash while she is being petted, and then call her back to you. Anyone who knows Gamine is acutely aware of how much she loves everyone she meets. It took some prompting on my part to convince her that I really was the better offer during that exercise. It is important to point out that the ever-enticing "treat in a pocket" is not allowed at a therapy dog test. If it were, that recall would have been a piece of cake. When I laugh at JJ's incredible skill at convincing people she's starving, it's obvious the apple does not fall far from the tree. While there are still plenty of people who leave food down for their dogs throughout the day, the concept of free feeding is simply not an option at our house.

This? This is not begging. This is being attentive to people's needs. This is saying: "I'm here for you. How can I help?" You might see something else, but this highly trained, intuitive hospice dog begs to differ!

I chose to do our volunteer visits with JJ at the assisted living facility where the stress level was lower to give her a chance to get used to her role.

At the same time, our hospice program was in the middle of building our new Hospice House. Since JJ would be working with me at this inpatient facility, I got in as many volunteer visits at the assisted living facility, and adjacent memory care unit, as I could, in preparation for her work role. She also could go on some hospice home visits, just as Callie used to, while we waited to transition to the inpatient unit. Right after passing her first therapy dog test, I took JJ and Mama Gamine into Samaritan's human resources department to get their own badges. JJ's photo turned out well, although Gamine's was a bit more DMV-like. I'm not sure how much JJ appreciated her badge because she promptly chewed on the first one she was given. It's fair to say puppies take a while to grow up, even when they seem to be mature! I had to return to human resources with the badge saying, "No really, the dog chewed it up," and they all got a laugh as they passed it around while we waited for the replacement. I still have that first badge because it makes me laugh and reminds me that at the end of the day, these wonderful souls are still just dogs.

Another volunteer day at memory care. We ran into one of the hospice social workers we know from our work that asked us to spend time with one of the residents. The message we got later said: "Thanks! Perfect timing. I have never been able to connect with that resident, and it was so awesome to see her smile with JJ, and to see her genuine pleasure in that interaction and the calling card you gave her! Thanks so much for giving her, and me, that gift!"

Early on in her puppy training visits, it became clear to me how intuitive JJ was. The three therapy dogs I had before her seemed quite instinctive as well, but nothing like JJ. Shortly after getting her Samaritan badge, JJ joined me at the nursing facility where we had done some of our early puppy training. I was our hospice's nurse for that home at the time. We had a conference scheduled with the facility's social worker and the wife—whom I will call Sandra—of a patient who was rapidly failing and having some complicated symptoms. I stood toward the side of the room, as the social worker was talking to Sandra. She had been holding it together for the sake of her husband, but tears were rolling down her face. JJ advanced toward Sandra, nudged her hands with her head, and then proceeded to lick the tears from her cheek. The social worker and I both pretty much lost it as we bore witness to such a touching and intimate moment of love and support. Sandra just hugged JJ and cried, while JJ stood patiently waiting. It was a time when words were inadequate, but the comfort of a dog was exactly what Sandra needed—and JJ was more than willing to provide it.

• • •

Once our Hospice House opened, JJ started working twelve-hour shifts with me. Just as I had seen the benefit of therapy dogs in the inpatient hospice setting, I knew it would be a great value here, not only to patients and families, but also to our visitors, staff, and volunteers. Generally, it would be frowned upon for a staff member to spend the day playing, sleeping, and begging from patients and families, but JJ was an ambassador of our hospice program as we prepared to open, so she had special privileges from day one. Honestly, we're all a wee bit jealous, as there are days a power nap sounds awfully good. She has her own crate in the nurses' station and all staff knows not to bother her there if she is sleeping. She only crates herself when she is very tired, or if for some reason I need her to be contained. For the most part, it is an oversized toy box. Our rule in crate training dogs is that their crate is their "safe place" where they won't be disturbed when they need to rest. The staff helps enforce this rule when she needs a break from visiting kids who keep trying to find her.

Our first year at the Hospice House was a time when JJ came into her own and became very confident in her work. For a while, she was still somewhat apprehensive around young children, but as you can imagine, we have had many, many children of all ages visit over the years. She has learned to read children and respond in an appropriate manner, though if she comes high-tailing it into the nurses' station with a child following, we know to intervene on her behalf. Some kids are just too exuberant in their interactions with dogs. We always have someone, whether myself or another staff member, keeping an eye on any interactions between JJ and kids, making sure it is a safe, positive visit. Very often it is an excellent opportunity to teach children how to safely approach and interact with dogs. We even have coloring and sticker books for kids that help teach them.

I'm learning! Not all kids are comfortable with dogs and the little girl was timid at first. I stayed perfectly still so I wouldn't scare her, and I got a great massage in the process!

Pets are allowed to visit patients at the Hospice House, but there are rules in place for everyone's safety. Just as therapy dogs are not allowed to visit with other dogs while "working," JJ and the other therapy dogs do not interact with visiting pets at the Hospice House. Animals absolutely know when something is wrong with their person, so the Hospice House can be a stressful environment for any visiting animal. When dogs are stressed, they are more apt to be grumpy, and the last thing we would ever want is a scuffle. JJ doesn't fight or argue with other dogs, but it's also about perception, even if it is simply a lip curl or a snarl from a visiting dog. JJ is one of the most neutral dogs I know, but I never want to take the risk, so it's best to use prevention and just not allow any interaction. One of the rules for a visiting pet is that the door to the room is to be kept closed, especially when JJ and I are working. As JJ makes her rounds, she almost always pops her head in the rooms just to check up on people. She knows she is not allowed into a room until I give her permission, but she is a curious dog with a great nose, so she knows exactly which room has a pet visiting. Keeping the door closed ensures a safe environment. There have been cases when people are quite insistent that their dog meet or play with JJ. In those instances, we have her stay in the nurses' station as dogs walk by and simply explain she's a working dog and cannot interact with their dog. There are occasions when she already knows the visiting dog, and at those times, we will go off the floor and let the dogs have some play time.

Ooh, ooh, ooh! Look who I found today! This is Amber, and I was her neutral dog last month at her Project Canine recertification. She is here with a patient, so I get to see her and her person throughout the day. I'm going to be Amber's therapy dog a little later so she can blow off some doggie steam, since they have been here for a while. Amber also has a Samaritan badge just like mine!

We live in a smaller community in Oregon, and because of this, it is not at all uncommon to hear someone say: "JJ, is that you?" when we are out running errands. In fact, many of these people are not sure what *my* name is. On the job, or even when volunteering where I know people, I am used to walking into the room behind my dog hearing, "Hi JJ. It's so good to see you" and only after a beat or two will I hear, "Oh, hi to you too, Tracy. Sorry." This was a common occurrence when Callie was alive as well. I confess to often remembering a dog's name better than its owner's, so I completely understand.

Still, when I was a new hospice nurse, and much younger without the life experience I now have, I found these run-ins with family members of former patients awkward. My presence seemed to remind them of a sad time and a painful loss, so it often felt uncomfortable. I am thankful that over time, these instances have gotten much easier and I have become much better at being present and reconnecting with people when I encounter them. Additionally, JJ helps. Being reminded of a loved one's death is often sad and difficult, however, the connection they had with JJ, and their memories of her, bring smiles to their faces. I am reminded every time how fortunate I am to have a partner like her.

Because JJ and I do so many different activities in our community now—be it hospice work, therapy dog visits, or crisis response callouts—it has become common for those seemingly separate worlds to overlap. In the past, I had never experienced a connection with my community in this way, and it leaves me with a good feeling. It is nice to be able to work with JJ to provide support to those in our community.

I was surprised to see one of the people I visit every other week at the local memory care center come into the Hospice House. It was quite bittersweet to tell her people how we knew her. But they agreed she has always been an animal lover. Things have changed so much since our visit to memory care this past Tuesday, but I got to snuggle on the bed with her and I gave my special hugs to her people. What a small world it is to be giving her loving caregivers support in my house as they visit her here.

3

When asked, "Did you tell your peeps that you wanted to pursue this career or did they suggest it to you?" I answer by saying it was something that I trained for. But early on I showed an interest in interacting with people in general. I passed my first therapy dog test on the day after I turned one. I'm told I am the most intuitive therapy dog she's had and so it has been a very good fit.

In this country, even though it is a relatively newer occurrence, we have become used to seeing animals used in therapy work. The benefits animals have on health were noted as early as the eighteenth century. In York, England, a Quaker named William Tuke took over one of the asylums for the mentally ill. He converted it with a goal of treating those with mental illness humanely rather than using brutal punishment to deal with those patients. The retreat setting he created was stocked with "various small domestic animals" for patients to interact with as one form of treatment. In *Notes on Nursing*, published in 1880, Florence Nightingale—the founder of modern nursing—highlighted how animals could have a unique power to heal. She wrote, "A small pet animal is often an excellent companion for the sick, for long chronic cases especially." Even Sigmund Freud was known to have his dog Jofi accompany him during psychotherapy sessions. He found she had a calming effect on patients, especially children, and they were more willing to talk openly with Jofi in the room. While these examples show how animals have been enhancing human health for a long time, the first formal therapy animal organization wasn't started until the 1970s in the United States.

In the past two decades, the use of animals in various settings has grown tremendously. There has been an increase in demand for pet therapy services across the country. Much of this can be attributed to the exposure of such services across mainstream and social media. Therapy dogs have become more widely accepted by the medical community as beneficial for stress relief and for assisting with therapeutic interactions. There now are a multitude of therapy animal organizations across the country, most of which are limited to dogs.

Dogs, however, were not my first exposure to Animal-Assisted Therapy—horses were. In 1990, I volunteered with a therapeutic riding program in Washington State called Little Bit Therapeutic Riding Center. I grew up with horses in Montana and found a kindred spirit with this program as an adult volunteer. The program had been in existence for about 14 years when I joined as a volunteer. At Little Bit, along with other therapeutic riding centers across the country, horses are used to improve the minds, bodies, and spirits of children and adults with disabilities. The movements of the horse help to improve coordination, balance, mobility, and self-confidence, to name a few things. I witnessed one of the young riders, who was wheelchair bound with mild contractures, sit up with her legs relaxed when on horseback. It was amazing to witness the smiles of the riders, and often their parents. We not only spent time in the arena, but would take the clients trail riding as well. Each horse had a volunteer leading them along, and one or two people were next to the rider supporting them physically as needed. As a volunteer, not only did I help during riding time, but I was also responsible for helping groom and tack up the horses before the session and putting them up afterward. I had missed being around horses and I loved being back around these gentle giants, breathing in the pungent odors and kissing their velvety noses. When I moved farther away and was no longer able to volunteer, I remembered this time fondly.

In the years since then, something called hippotherapy developed. It is the formal use of equine therapy in physical, occupational, or speech therapy with the goal of achieving a functional outcome. Therapeutic riding still exists and defines the recreational riding for those with disabilities, while hippotherapy focuses on using horses to achieve individual therapeutic goals.

Once I had dogs in my life again as an adult, I was pleased to find I could continue the volunteer work I did with horses with a smaller, more portable, animal partner. Reading that article in the news about dogs in therapy work had inspired me to join a national organization and start work with my dog Booker. But in 2013, one year after the Hospice House opened and shortly before it was time to re-test JJ's therapy dog evaluation, I was introduced to Project Canine, which is based out of Seattle with some teams in Oregon as well. Project Canine's Connecting Canines program was started with the goal of setting the gold standard in Animal-Assisted Therapy team education, training, certification, and outreach. Teams receive hands-on training from experienced trainers and, after completing the certification process, all teams are covered by Project Canine's liability insurance for volunteer therapy dog visits. Project Canine is the only program that requires continuing education as a part of recertification, with testing every two years. They offer puppy certifications and puppy partnerships, as well as special endorsements for experienced teams. Project Canine's core philosophy believes that dogs that feel safe and supported by knowledgeable, attentive handlers can improve the lives of those they visit. I found their philosophy was well suited to mine, and it was clear this was a better fit for me than the larger, national therapy dog organization I had started with so many years before.

Two years later, I got involved by helping with the testing process for new Project Canine teams and was invited to go through the process of becoming a licensed instructor and examiner. Along with training and testing, we were also required to participate in continuing education. It has been a fun process to become a part of our organization and watch new teams learn.

As a therapy dog handler and examiner, one of the first things I learned was to determine if a prospective therapy dog was even suited for the job. Not all dogs are appropriate for therapy work, and that's perfectly OK. Think about a parent who dreams of his child becoming an NFL quarterback, while all along that kid has a passion for dance and couldn't care less about sports. While it is very common for dogs to give love and joy to their own people, it is much less typical for the average dog to want to initiate contact with a stranger. Therapy dogs must be able to be calm in their interactions, especially around small children, the elderly, or anyone who is fragile. JJ's sire Dash loved humans and getting petted, but he would scare the be-jeebers out of people with his exuberant talking and smiling (causing him to easily be perceived as an aggressive dog). He was overly animated in his desire to interact with people, and would spin in excited circles, making his way toward someone he wanted to greet. Picture the smiling, talking, happy dog (read: a snarling, growly hot mess of a hairy beast ready to take someone out at the knees mid-spin) just trying to get some love. Even at thirteen, his spirited style never diminished. He certainly made us all happy, but clearly would never have been a good fit for the job JJ excels at. But he found his place too; he loved competing in retriever field games and was an AKC Master Hunter.

When I first started with Booker, I had to learn about canine body language. It is amazing to learn the rich communication skills of both subtle and overt signs that dogs use to try to convey to their people and other dogs that they are stressed. These are called calming signals and are used to help a dog relax itself and those who are the cause of the stress, in the hopes of de-escalating the situation and avoiding having to act aggressively. Calming signals include yawning, lip licking, sniffing, looking away, and play bows, to name a few. Unfortunately, many times owners don't know how to listen to their dogs. When dogs have been pushed too far and calming signals aren't working, they will resort to aggression, which can include biting. Owners sometimes argue that the bite comes "out of the blue," but dogs spend a lot of time trying to communicate their stress before resorting to a physical reaction.

When the stress escalates, dogs may exhibit signs such as panting, barking or whining, showing the whites of the eyes, tucking their tail, shaking, freezing in place, and even showing sweaty paws. Once I learned the nuances of dog language, it was not hard to pick out the calming signals all dogs put off. When JJ is starting to feel some stress, she will yawn repeatedly and pant, sometimes heavily. She also will tuck her tail and if it remains tucked, I know she is past the point of needing a timeout. The key for me is to watch and give her a break before the stress escalates. If a dog continually works in stressful environments without enough breaks and time off, not only is it ethically wrong to do, but the dog is very likely to stop wanting to interact with people altogether.

With my prospective therapy dogs being of any age, I start with socialization—exposure to people, dogs, and novel situations—as well as basic obedience, since any therapy dog needs to be well mannered when out in public. Everyone has probably had the experience of being around an out of control dog with a less than attentive handler—it does not leave a good impression. Even if the dog is genuinely affectionate and loves people, having that dog pull its handler along, as though they were an Iditarod sled team, shows a remarkable lack of control. Exuberance in a dog is not cute when the animal is invading people's personal space, and it reflects an owner's lack of respect and lack of control of their pet. For example, letting your dog run up to greet a stranger and letting it jump up to get a little love while you say, "It's OK, he's friendly," can be a nightmare for that stranger even if they like dogs. Far more impressive to the general public is a dog that can maneuver in a public setting with a calm demeanor while obeying any commands given by its handler.

When new potential teams come to our Project Canine preparation class, they learn about therapy dog fundamentals and how to prepare for the exam with their dog. It is a four-hour class, and it gives us a chance to watch how dog and handler react to different stimuli. There also is the opportunity for the handler and dog to practice the different parts of the test, including the exposure to medical equipment such as a walker and wheelchair—common items experienced during therapy dog visits. We always have one or two dogs, called the neutral dogs, relaxing in the room as we monitor how the potential therapy dogs react to a strange dog in the proximity. The second time we evaluate the response to a neutral dog is during the test.

People often ask about the purpose of this in our testing. When I am out in a public setting making volunteer visits, it is common to run into someone with a dog. It is important for therapy dogs to remain well behaved and under control in these circumstances. They do not interact with other dogs while visiting, but all dogs are very much aware of one another, even if they are not next to each other. When we evaluate potential teams, the testing dog must be able to walk calmly next to the handler while approaching another person with a dog (the neutral dog). To pass the therapy test, the dog cannot be overly friendly and want to greet the other dog or show signs of any aggressive behavior. They just need to stay calm and well mannered while the people pause, greet each other, and then move on. Project Canine treats the components of the therapy dog test as real life. During this testing, I can talk to my dog and settle her before talking to the other person. JJ has come a long way from that first therapy dog test when we barely passed the neutral dog portion. She is now one of our primary dogs used for this portion of the testing. JJ's ability to be a calm neutral dog has been extremely helpful at the Hospice House as well, since our patients can have their personal pets visit.

Another example of "neutral dog" importance. I know to boot-scoot into the nurses' station when another dog comes in. Pets are often stressed when they come into my second home. Even when their people do not recognize the signs, it can be hard for animals to come into an unknown place with many different smells, sights, and sounds.

A unique element of our Project Canine therapy dog testing is the assessment of resource guarding. This is the term used for dogs who demonstrate possessive and/or aggressive behavior toward other animals or people to convince them to stay away from a desired item. It can be food, treats, toys, a favorite spot, or even a person. We see this behavior over and over with our home hospice patients and their dogs. These dogs are already stressed because they are aware something is seriously wrong with their owner, and then perfect strangers start entering their home day after day. Nurses and hospice aides who are touching the person while giving care are most at risk of being nipped or bitten, which is why we usually have a plan to have the dog in a different area of the house during a hospice home visit. It is perfectly understandable how a dog in this situation might be protective, so the best thing to do is to prevent anything from ever happening. Potential therapy dogs must be able to tolerate strangers interacting with their handler. We first evaluate this early in the testing process by reaching over the dog and hugging the handler. The number of dogs who do not like their people being touched might surprise people. My partner Amy and I alternate roles between tester and scribe during our testing of teams. As a hands-on tester, I am looking for any stress signs the dog is exhibiting during each exercise. Later, we discuss what signs the handler notices in their dog when he or she is stressed, and then we compare what we noticed during testing. The goal is to raise awareness for our therapy dog handlers so they can best advocate for their dogs.

The second method of testing for resource guarding is with tasty food. It is most fun for the dogs who are food motivated. We place several small treats out in front of them, have their handler say "OK," and then proceed to shuffle and pick up some of the pieces around them while they eat to make sure they are not protective. Afterward, we give them something of high value, such as a bully stick, and then take it from them in exchange for another treat. For safety's sake, we want to make sure the dogs we pass will not exhibit resource guarding. This part of the test is JJ's absolute favorite and she is always ready to "practice" when I am working at home with one of my puppies or dogs on this.

One of the most practiced exercises prior to therapy dog testing is "leave it." This is a command that is taught to tell the dog to avoid something, such as food or medication dropped on the floor. There is no way to know if something the dog wants to put in its mouth is a hazard, so it's best to treat anything in this regard as potentially harmful. When we test, we squeak a toy with the dog watching and set it on the floor. The handler must walk the dog past the toy without allowing them to pick up the toy. Impulse control in this situation can be quite challenging with a high-drive dog. "Leave it" is the exercise JJ is least impressed with. I periodically practice by putting treats on her paws and not letting her have them until I give her the OK. She's quite good with giving me a side-eye stare during these times.

• • •

The topic of hugging dogs has been discussed extensively in the dog therapy and training world. Most dogs would much prefer a belly rub or a good scratch on their hind end to being hugged. People may see hugging as a sign of affection, but this human attribute does not necessarily translate to our dogs. Dogs don't put a leg over another in friendly affection, but rather as a method of control in a show of dominance. While there are plenty of dogs that will tolerate a hug from a stranger, most simply are not comfortable with this. It's also one thing for a dog to snuggle with his owner on his terms, while completely another when a random stranger drapes their arms around a dog's neck, often in a tight squeeze. While we coach therapy dog handlers to be proactive and manage visits, including preventing the dog from being hugged, sometimes it happens quickly during a visit without warning. Therapy dogs must be reliable in tolerating a restraining hug. Some people in other groups have advocated removing the restraining hug from the therapy dog evaluation process because so many dogs don't like it, but we need to make sure all dogs we certify can safely handle such an instance. Dog owners often mention to me that their dog does just fine with hugs, but usually the owners aren't able to see his or her expression, including any stress signals the dog is trying to give off. When we have practiced this in our therapy dog preparation class, I often will take either videos or photos to show handlers how their dog reacts. Very often the response is, "I would not have guessed my dog's reaction. I thought he liked it."

This is an example of a restraining hug, which also falls under the exuberant, clumsy petting category and why therapy dogs must be able to pass this portion of a test. It happens a lot, especially in hospice work. Please keep in mind, many dogs need space, so having someone put their face close to a dog's face, especially children, could spell disaster for all involved. This was allowed simply to get a photo of such a hug.

As a therapy dog handler, the most important thing for me to keep in mind is that I am my dog's advocate, and she comes first. I once watched an eye-opening video taken from a dog's point of view, while he and his handler visited a nursing home. The camera was mounted on a harness on the dog's back. I have a three-foot advantage over my dog and can see down the hallway or over the nurse's station, so am less likely to be surprised by things we encounter. However, even I was startled to see a wheelchair come whipping around a corner from the dog's viewpoint and I realized I jumped a little during the video. It also seemed extraordinarily busy from the dog's point of view, with many different things approaching him throughout the video. I recognize how easily I can tune things out on a busy floor, especially because I am used to that kind of environment as a nurse. Because of this, it's important for me to be paying attention to what my dog encounters and even try to think ahead to what she will be seeing. As a handler, one of the most important things I have learned is to be in tune with the end of my leash. Meaning, my dog can get in trouble if I am not paying attention to her and any stress signs she exhibits. Dogs do their best to use their body language to tell people when they are not happy. My primary job is to pay attention to what JJ is trying to tell me, and then to decrease the stress she is feeling.

Once I became a handler, I discovered my job wasn't done and I still needed to socialize and expose my dog to different elements in the world. I consider it continuing education and lifelong learning not only for me, but also for my canine partner. Early on, JJ went out and about a lot with me and I thought I was doing a fairly good job of introducing her to different things. A couple of years ago we went to one of the local universities for a therapy dog event. As we walked from the parking lot to the heart of campus, some students whizzed by on skateboards and JJ nearly went straight up the nearest tree. It never even dawned on me to introduce her to skateboarders, and I'm quite certain she is convinced they are invaders from another planet. Surprise novelty experiences are a time when high-value treats are good to have on hand! To this day I'm not sure she is terribly thrilled when we stumble upon a skateboarder, but I've worked to simply desensitize her to them so she doesn't feel she is going to come out of her skin. Motorcyclists wearing helmets are also never to be trusted, in her humble opinion. That one is a bit more difficult to try to manage, since I am usually chauffeuring her somewhere when she pronounces great danger is approaching. Sometimes, you just need to pick your battles.

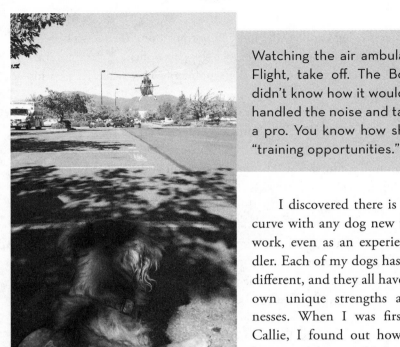

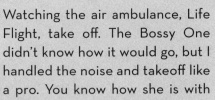

Watching the air ambulance, Life Flight, take off. The Bossy One didn't know how it would go, but I handled the noise and takeoff like a pro. You know how she is with "training opportunities."

I discovered there is a learning curve with any dog new to therapy work, even as an experienced handler. Each of my dogs has been very different, and they all have had their own unique strengths and weaknesses. When I was first training Callie, I found out how awkward her attentions could be. She had been a mother and a nanny and was always very attentive to young puppies, whether they were her own or someone else's. During a therapy dog preparation class, we took all the dogs from class to a local mall to expose them to novel situations and different people. This was the first time I had Callie around young children, and I found out how vigilant she really was, no matter the species. A woman was pushing a stroller with a crying baby and Callie went on high alert. We were close by and it was clear Callie wanted to check on the baby, because when she was around tiny puppies, she would always check them and clean them if necessary. I had visions of Callie snuffling around this baby, trying to get closer for cleanup duty. She was doing her best to pull me toward the sounds of the cries, and the mother looked up, a bit startled as I was trying to redirect Callie. I had her sit next to my side, smiled, and explained to the woman that Callie had been a very attentive mother and she was most concerned about the baby's distress. It was obvious to the mother that Callie was only curious and was no threat, and she laughingly offered to let her babysit. I hadn't expected Callie to react this way to a human baby, but the experience taught me to keep treats in my pocket for any random babies, dogs, or other animals we might run into. This strategy has worked for all my dogs, since all have been very treat motivated and distracted quickly by the offer of a cookie. Luckily, as much as JJ loves being a puppy nanny, she doesn't react quite as strongly as Callie did to a crying baby and I can manage the interaction easily. JJ will show some concern, but I don't have to deal with the extremely awkward situation Callie would try to put us in. I have also learned to just roll with things. As long as I have a pocketful of treats, we can pretty much handle anything. New learning opportunities seem to present themselves all the time.

When dealing with little people or little animals, it is best to get down on their level. I am by no means a big girl, but it's very calming and non-threatening when I am in a down position. For those with larger therapy dogs, try this during your visits anytime you encounter someone who appears apprehensive because of the dog's size. It can be a helpful trick for children and adults alike. Bitsy, a teeny tiny Yorkie, wanted to say hi to me, but big dogs scare her, so my downward dog worked like a charm! Isn't she cute? I work with her Mom.

4

When a patient dies, very often the family's goodbyes involve so many of our talented staff members. While one family was gathered around, our music therapist played her harp and the family serenaded their mother with hymns. Afterward, I stood close by her daughter, finally putting my head on her knee to let her know I was there for her. To make her Walkout unique, I picked up my pink dinosaur toy that was just outside her door as I led the way out. Her people smiled and chuckled through their tears. My people were told their mother would have just loved it.

That's JJ describing one of her more memorable Walkouts. When someone dies at our facility, we honor that person and their loved ones with a formal ceremony called the Walkout—escorting the body out the same front door they came in. It's a way of saying to the patient, "You meant something in this world, and whether or not we knew you, we honor you." This ritual must be one of the most touching and heart-wrenching aspects of care we provide at the Hospice House, whether experienced in person or shared through stories. Any staff members on site during this time will line the hallways in respect, standing quietly while our music therapist's harp plays in the background. We have had special quilts made to drape the gurney for this ceremony—a special one for veterans and another for non-veterans. Our Walkouts happen with every death, whether or not family members choose to stay and participate. On a busy weekday when many of the outpatient hospice staff are in the building, we can have up to fifty staff members lining the halls. The nature of the work at our inpatient hospice facility involves many deaths and Walkouts, sometimes several in a day. While we get used to the reality of death, there is something about looking up during a Walkout and seeing so many people marking this moment for the person who has just died that it will bring tears to everyone's eyes. Sometimes, this show of respect is overwhelming to loved ones. I often hear from our staff that for them, very often the most touching part is the role JJ plays during this ceremony.

I had no part in training JJ to do the things she does during the Walkout. She has become a sort of standard-bearer (she took this responsibility on herself). According to staff members who witnessed her first effort, she'd been sitting outside the patient room in the hallway, quietly waiting while we were in the room preparing for the very first Walkout of our facility. As the funeral director pushed the gurney into the hallway, JJ stood up and walked next to the gurney, escorting it all the way outside to the waiting van. This was not a fluke—she has continued this tradition with each Walkout we have been in the building to participate in. Some times while we prepare, she spends time comforting grieving families outside the room—passing out hugs and asking for belly rubs. Occasionally, she'll come into the room with us, and if a family member has chosen to stay in the room, she'll wait with that person, providing comfort. She decides for herself what she thinks she should do in each situation, and we trust her judgment. There have been sometimes when I don't even know where she is when I go into the room to help prepare the body. However, once we open the door to come out for the Walkout, there she is, waiting patiently with her head resting on her paws, facing the direction we will walk.

Over the years, JJ has found ways to change things up, sometimes surprising us. But I am astounded at the way her intuitive nature has always grasped the right behavior. Recently during a Walkout, instead of walking next to the gurney, she stayed a few steps back and walked right next to the daughter of our patient. The woman had been having a difficult time, and JJ obviously sensed where she was needed. Another time, she stayed next to an extremely distraught partner as he did his best to cope with the loss of his love. JJ was very concerned about him, and she walked next to him out the door and waited while he said a brief goodbye. When he abruptly turned and walked off to his car, she stayed glued to his side all the way through the parking lot. She even sat for a while, holding her ground, after he got in his car. We were all a bit in shock over this, as she has never been so focused in this way on one person during a Walkout. Fortunately, the funeral home driver was paying attention so he didn't hit her, but she seemed to be in a daze and I had to call her to get her back inside. Because of her inexplicable behavior, one of the nurses phoned the partner that evening to check on him, another thing that isn't usually done. He was doing as well as could be expected, and our bereavement staff made sure to follow up with him quickly to ensure he had support. To this day, we still don't know what had so absorbed JJ. The secret remains hers.

The first time JJ grabbed a toy—a pink dragon no less—for a Walkout, I was surprised and a little concerned about the change in tenor. After three years of more solemn Walkouts, she was abruptly making it more interesting and light-hearted. But then, to my relief, I heard from the patient's daughter later how tickled her mother would have been to know JJ accompanied her with the toy that JJ used to bring to her room when she was alive. In fact, our hospice received a letter afterward from the granddaughter of the deceased detailing the family's appreciation and mentioning JJ in particular: "Thanks for taking such good care of my grandmother and grandfather. They are huge dog lovers and knowing they had JJ there to make them feel loved makes all the difference. Thank you, thank you, thank you."

We serve a small community, and it is not at all uncommon to take care of spouses over time. Since families can bring their pets to the Hospice House to visit, not only do we recognize family members we have served before, but we recognize their pets as well. While JJ does not interact with most visiting pets, some have been able to go off the floor with her to have some supervised play, especially when pets have been visiting for a while. The environment and circumstances can be stressful for these pets as well, so the break can be good for them. There's one younger yellow Lab, Kirby, who spent time with JJ in play therapy while we cared for his owner's father. Eighteen months later, his owner's mother was dying and they were with us again. JJ and Kirby clearly recognized each other and were eager for more play therapy. When the time came for this family's Walkout, there was a bit of lightheartedness to it. As one person noted, "You know, not everyone wants it somber when they transition. If JJ and Kirby were revved a bit, then JJ knew. She always seems spot on."

The wait for the actual Walkout to begin can be difficult. Most of the time, JJ will spend time in the hallway with loved ones, providing comfort and sometimes comic relief. Our bereavement counselor often hears stories about JJ's method of comforting family members when she follows up with them. Many are delighted when JJ sits up and wraps her paws around their hand or arm, usually looking at the face of the person she is interacting with. This unique comforting style is another thing that has been self-taught by JJ. With a regular therapy dog, you would not let them put their paws up on someone on their own initiative, though it can be taught as a command to be performed when the handler recognizes it is appropriate. However, at the Hospice House, JJ spends most of her time off leash, so I would not be able to reinforce a command like this. It was abundantly clear from early on how much people enjoy JJ's "hugs." Sometimes, she will balance on her haunches and cross both front paws over someone's arm and sometimes she places each paw on the upper arm of the person crouched down and will tuck her head into the person. People get an amazed smile on their faces. Because of these interactions, many family members remember JJ's name, while forgetting the names of human staff members.

We started the day on call, and when we were called in, we walked in two minutes after someone had just died. TBO went her way and I went mine, as is typical when I come in after a few days off. This person's daughter was sobbing in the hall, so I went up and spent time with her, giving her hugs and comfort. She hadn't met me before and kept saying to staff, "She's hugging me!" I then spent time with the rest of the family. It was one of those times that makes all my work people a little misty eyed. As we all prepared when the funeral director arrived, a different family member wanted me to visit, but she was told I would be busy doing a Walkout right then. This family member was quite insistent that a dog couldn't know or have the intuition to know such a thing. As the day went on, their nurse told some of my stories, TBO answered many of their questions, and they ended up being quite amazed and open to the idea that a dog could be intuitive about the end of life.

When JJ has spent a significant amount of time comforting family members, sometimes they are not prepared for the emotion elicited when she participates in the Walkout. We always ask the loved ones if they want the person's face covered or not. As in everything we do with hospice, we individualize our care to the preferences of the person and family. All families are given a lavender candle in remembrance of their loved one, courtesy of one local mom as a way of honoring the son she lost. He died at an inpatient hospice facility in a different state, and she was given a lavender candle in tribute to him. When we were preparing to open the Hospice House, she reached out to us and offered to provide candles. Families are incredibly touched by this gesture, as well as the candle that is lit at the nurses' station for 24 hours after their loved one has died. Due to the generosity of local quilt groups, we can give each patient their own special quilt when they arrive at the Hospice House. Family members are given the quilt that rested on the bed, so they can take home something that was close to that person before he or she died. We do prepare visitors when a Walkout is about to happen, in case they do not want to be around to witness it. In a touching gesture of community support, often visitors and other patients' family members will stop what they are doing and join in the tribute for this person who has just died. The combination of the harp music, staff, and visitors standing quietly on each side of the hall, along with JJ's presence at the side of the gurney, is so appreciated by our families. As one wife remembers, "Yes, such a special dog. Forever in my memory, walking my sweetheart out."

Sometimes the Walkouts are not only draining on families, but on staff as well. As one of my colleagues has said, "Our Walkouts can be very hard to do, but seeing such compassion from an animal as sweet as JJ is a Godsend. The families and staff always appreciate her appearance and form of comfort she gives. We feel her presence during a Walkout is very therapeutic to everyone involved during that special but sad time." I have been told by several of our hospice staff the sight of JJ walking next to the gurney is the thing that will bring them to tears.

Since the first pink dinosaur Walkout, she has occasionally brought a toy along, but decides for herself when this is necessary. None of this is directed; I have accepted that she always seems to know what is appropriate to the mood. When she does have a toy with her, the staff just smiles and shakes their heads at her. Toy or no toy, "JJ brings calmness and peace to the Walkout, continuing her support right up until it is time for the physical body to leave." We are all proud and honored to do the work we do, and JJ's representation of this honor for all of us as she leads the procession down the hall and outside speaks volumes to all.

I am never sure what is going to happen when we leave the doors to approach the waiting van in the parking lot. On many occasions, Syd, the cat, would be standing by waiting, and JJ walks right by him. I used to worry they would get into an argument, but thankfully they never have. Sometimes JJ will walk up to the van and wait patiently as the gurney is loaded. At other times, there is a butterfly or bird needing to be chased or she decides to run a couple of laps. The silliness of these antics provides some lighthearted moments for families. We always tell people the gamut of emotions they feel are appropriate and healthy. I learned early to trust JJ and not interfere unless she gets totally crazy. Trying to figure out the rhyme and reason behind what she does would drive me mad. Clearly therapy dogs like to have some secrets.

There are times when families have been present at the Hospice House for days on end, and thus, often will have witnessed at least one Walkout. Since JJ only works twelve-hour shifts with me and is not in the building at all times, it can be disappointing when she isn't there to participate. During one family's long goodbye, I could tell our patient was getting close to death. When we get to know family members well, I always hope JJ can participate in those Walkouts. This gentleman finally died early the next morning. I heard his daughter and grandson had wished JJ could have been there, as they had watched her participate in several Walkouts the week prior. However, Sydney, the therapy cat, was waiting at the front door to greet them as they walked him out.

On occasion, if there is a great need for a pet therapy visit, we have gone into the Hospice House on our day off, but I try to keep this to a minimum because JJ and I need our rest on days off.

The Hospice House is a place where people die. Part of our job is to normalize it a bit and make the process a bit less scary. As sad as it can be, none of us get out of this journey, and the wonderful paid and unpaid staff here (as well as so many who serve our home patients) spend a large amount of time preparing our families for this process. When I share Walkout stories, it is one of the most touching things for people to read, especially when JJ's role is included. We all must say goodbye at some time in our lives and by sharing, the intent is to educate others about the end of life and to get people thinking.

A couple of years ago, a reporter and photographer from the local newspaper came to the Hospice House to do a story on the hospice therapy dogs. JJ and I happened to be working that day—a Thursday, which is when the entire outpatient hospice staff meets every week. We made sure the other dogs, Marfa, a Lab-Border Collie mix, and Phoebe, a Cardigan Corgi, could be there as well. It was a chaotic day with a mostly full house, including one patient who was actively dying. The reporter wanted some family perspective of the support provided by therapy dogs at the end of life, and it turned out that the daughter of one of the other patients was willing to be interviewed and photographed with one of the hospice dogs. While that group was in another room, JJ and I were in the room with the patient who was dying peacefully, surrounded by family members. As it happens when so many people are in the building for a Walkout, we had at least forty people lining the hallways for this person's Walkout, including the newspaper staff, who were in awe of the powerful experience. The resulting front-page story not only had local residents reading about the therapy dogs' work, but the article was picked up by the *Associated Press* and run online across the country. I had several people, including patients' family members we have cared for in the past, contact me to let me know they had read it.

Our hospice program is one of the many across the country that participates in something called We Honor Veterans. Currently, approximately one-fourth of all people in this country who die in hospice are veterans. The goal of the partnership between hospice programs and the We Honor Veterans program is to educate providers and staff in recognizing the unique needs of veterans and their families at end of life. We have flags from each branch of the service, and if the patient or family wants to have their service recognized, the flag is hung outside the patient's room's door to acknowledge that they are a veteran. In those cases, the flag is given to the family members when their loved one dies and we also use our Veterans Walkout quilt to recognize their service during our ceremony. As with everything we do, we individualize our care and follow a patient or family's wishes to the end.

We had the Walkout of a veteran this afternoon. As we prepared for the ceremony, the special quilt made for our veterans was placed over the gurney. Thank you for your service, sir. Your family will miss you, but your wife has been waiting for you for fifteen years. Now you both can watch over your people.

Formal occasions marking the rites of passage in our society seem to be fading to a casual nod, if noted at all. So many people now say, "Don't give me a funeral," or "I don't want anything done." When I started in hospice twenty-three years ago, it was more common to have funerals or memorials. Even for our staff who will attend funerals at times, it is difficult to hear that nothing is planned, not even a casual family get together. We are used to pivotal life events—births, graduations, and marriages—having some acknowledgement, if not a formal gathering. For some of our families, our Walkout is the only form of ceremony they will have as a way of saying the final goodbye. For staff, it is our chance to take a few minutes and recognize the life and death of the person being wheeled out of our facility.

It will continue to be our way of saying: "You mattered and are respected." Watching JJ participate reminds us of the comfort and love brought by this very special dog to everyone who has been touched by the journey of dying at this very special place.

5

The Samaritan Evergreen Hospice House opened for our first hospice patients in August 2012. We were the third inpatient hospice program in Oregon to build such a facility for hospice patients. While we were in the midst of building the Hospice House, JJ passed her first therapy dog evaluation and started doing formal volunteer and hospice therapy dog visits in preparation of becoming my full-time partner at the Hospice House. Once the building was completed, we held our open houses as we prepared for our first survey. Not only did we need to obtain our certificate of occupancy, we were required to receive a passing score from the surveyors before our first patients could be admitted. While we worked for a month on preparing policies and procedures, JJ got to explore her new second home. She seemed to figure out very quickly which offices had the dog treats, and it didn't take her long to develop a mooching route. She also loved seeing all the outpatient staff coming and going as we all adjusted to a new routine.

As I talked to people in the community while we were building the Hospice House, the usual questions would pop back up about the nature of hospice work. We are all used to the question, "Isn't that just so depressing?" and "I don't know how you do it. You must be an angel." If it was depressing, we wouldn't be able to do end of life care day after day. There are times when it is difficult and intense beyond belief, but thankfully, not every day. It's like being a midwife at the other end of the life cycle, and we have an amazing staff who help guide patients and families through this journey, both at our inpatient facility and out in the community. We also are not angels, simply people who are comfortable working with those who are dying. Death is a part of life and it's our job to normalize the things that happen during the dying process. Hospice not only cares for the person who is dying, but they also equally care for the person's loved ones. This work certainly is not for everyone, and how wonderful is that! We wouldn't get much done in this world if we all wanted to do the same thing. I know I am very grateful for the driver who picks up my garbage every week, the teacher who educates the young in our community, and the clerk who helps me make purchases at retail outlets.

Across the country, hospice facilities are used differently depending on the licensing and focus of care. Our inpatient facility was built specifically to provide intense, short-term care when someone's symptoms were out of control and required nursing attention and intervention twenty-four hours a day. We also have beds for something called respite—a component of hospice care for patients that are declining but still have a ways to go—in order to provide caregivers a break for up to five days. The building has offices for our in-home hospice staff as well. Over time, our admissions criteria have been adjusted as we make decisions on how those on our hospice program are best served. Through it all, JJ has remained my work partner. I am grateful to be a nurse who is in the unique position of having my dog come to work with me. What a blessing this has been! I am reminded time and time again how much she makes my job as a hospice nurse easier, and I love to share JJ stories and hear from family members how JJ has touched them.

While the Hospice House is JJ's second home, we have developed guidelines to make her interactions enjoyable for all. People don't have to visit with her, and we respect when she indicates she does not want to visit herself. In addition, there are urgent reasons why some rooms need to be off limits to JJ, such as when someone has an allergy or a dislike of dogs, or if the person is on isolation precautions. JJ has learned to wait for permission to enter a room the first time from me. If it is a new person, she will not enter if family or even staff tries to tell her it's OK to go in until I give her the green light—though she might poke her head around the door just to see what is happening. I often must stop what I am doing and make rounds with her so she can visit those who want to meet her. My nursing tasks are often far less meaningful than spending time with JJ and watching her comfort patients and family.

There are times when there are intense emotions or large amounts of family members gathered. JJ is very intuitive and will soak in those emotions as she seeks out those who need her. We hear all the time, "I don't know how she knows that I need her right now," from families and even staff. These highly charged emotional times are brief and intermittent, thank goodness. For those who don't do hospice work, it can be a surprise to learn that it is not oppressively depressing at our facility 24/7. JJ keeps the mood light and reminds us all to take breaks. Her preference is that our brief breaks involve something like playing with her, feeding her a cookie, or ignoring our silly paperwork so we can pet her. It is common to hear the comment: "I don't know who is getting more therapy right now, me or JJ."

The spectrum of emotions is normal in life and in death. There are times to smile, cry, be silly, temporarily withdraw, laugh, play, acknowledge heartache, and sometimes just put one's head down to get through the day. Many times, having a dog around helps to break down barriers individuals are up against in dealing with difficult things. For many, the presence alone of an animal can dramatically decrease stress, even when there is no petting involved. I have heard many visitors comment that simply seeing JJ in the building makes it feel more like home and puts them more at ease.

Our Hospice House has twelve beds, and when we first opened, it was new to everyone—including myself—as it had been eighteen years since I had done any inpatient work. While we are a part of our local hospital, our building is four miles away, and it was up to management and staff to figure out how to operate day to day. We needed be as flexible as Gumby and take it slow to get through the early phases. For the first six months we used only six of the rooms and operated with half of the staff we now have. As is typical of a place like this, food was involved, and JJ quickly learned how much she loved her new job and crowned herself Queen of Quality Control during mealtimes. Now, many of our hospice patients are minimally responsive or have very poor appetites, but during our first week, we started with respite patients only. Most of the time our respite patients do eat and, true to her hunting dog pedigree, JJ could follow the cone of scent and pinpoint the location after a meal was delivered to a room. These days, if I notice she's been gone for a bit, I ask who might be eating or check the staff's break room at lunchtime.

During the first two weeks, we had a home patient come in for symptom management. It became clear to us she was what we call "actively dying," where she had only hours to maybe a day left to live. We gave her family members as much TLC as we could, while making sure she was comfortable. One of the family members came back to the Hospice House with pizza and walked down to the room. JJ was lounging in the nurses' station, and as the pizza box passed down the hallway, her nose went straight up into the air and she was gone. When I got down to the room, there she was in front of the family in her best mooching pose. As I apologized to them and called her away, they just laughed. The starving therapy dog's antics were just the release they needed at a very sad time. Later, a family member shared a photo and story of JJ doing her absolute best to look cute and starving, while managing to convince her she needed some fries. We weren't working when her grandmother had her Walkout, but JJ was left presents of toys and treats in appreciation.

A few weeks after this, one of our hospice patients celebrated her birthday with us. She told her sister she wished she were healthy enough to go to Red Robin to eat. Her sister had a contact at the local franchise, and we had a visit from them a couple of days later with a special dinner for our patient. I wasn't sure how JJ would do with Red, the mascot. This was long before I ever knew about Animal Assisted Crisis Response work and, had it been on my radar, this would have been a perfect training opportunity. As it was, the giant red bird bearing heavenly gifts didn't faze her in the least. It really was a special moment for our patient and was fun for us to witness. JJ loved it as our patient adored her and was very fond of sneaking her human food, no matter what her silly owner had to say about it.

JJ is very well known for her mooching skills. While the staff has gotten good at ignoring her pleas, visitors often have a hard time resisting her insistent, cute face. She's no dummy and has plenty of patience. She does have a cookie jar in the lobby that I fill with the teeniest, tiniest dog biscuits I can find. Often, I will fill a medicine cup with them for families or patients to hand out to her instead of pieces of their lunch. We did have one gentleman who came in frequently for medication adjustment to control his cancer pain. JJ spent a lot of time with him, especially around mealtime. After he died, his wife shared a story with me about how much of a kick he got from tricking the CNAs into recording that he'd enjoyed his meal and, "cleaned his plate," when he had a very poor appetite. Apparently, Miss

JJ was in on the subterfuge and would help with much of the meal. It's a darned good thing that dog has an iron stomach. On another occasion, JJ was quick to lighten the mood for a family as their loved one was getting close to dying. One evening, she kept going back into the room, lingering. They were thinking that JJ knew something they didn't about our patient, although it didn't take long for them to realize she was interested in the burger and fries they had.

I am pretty sure The Bossy One is onto me. She gave everyone medicine cups filled with my biscuits (TINY ones, mind you) instead of "junk" food! I believe "junk" is in the mind of the beholder. Behold, I see bacon, manna from above and not junky in the least.

We worked one memorable Thanksgiving that saw not one, but two families celebrate in the building with huge feasts. I'm certain JJ thought she had hit the jackpot, although she was a well-behaved mooch and stayed away from the tables packed with food. There were kids of all ages everywhere, along with several sympathetic adults. Let's just say she got about ten pieces of kibble that night for dinner, compensating for her intake at work. While people food isn't very good for dogs, JJ certainly lightened the mood for so many that holiday. It is always hard to have to say goodbye to a loved one, yet there is something even more heartbreaking about saying goodbye during the holiday season. One family member was amazed at JJ's ability to home in on the one of them who had just said their goodbyes and was having a very difficult time. While everyone in the room was teary, JJ seemed to sense that that woman needed her the most at that moment. This was one of those times when JJ had made her rounds and I was not in the room, but the family shared the story with us all afterward. As is typical in hospice work, many people die between Thanksgiving and just after New Year's. This is a pattern borne out year after year, and my fellow hospice workers across the country experience the same thing. During this particular holiday stretch, we had five or six candles lit at the nurses' station at one time, and all of us, JJ included, were exhausted and a bit shell-shocked. Thank goodness these days are not common. It is far more typical to have one or two candles, if any, burning on a given day. The slower days balance our work and help us all relax a bit, recharge, and spend more quality time with our patients and families.

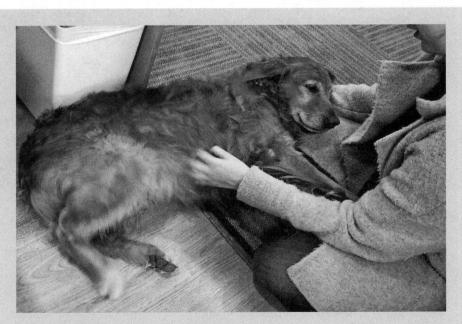

Now, it might look to you as if I am slacking off, but I am hard at work helping our families. Good massages just happen to come with this support, and spending time on the floor with me is good medicine.

We all venture through our lives with different outlooks and philosophies. Those of us in hospice work are careful to take a neutral stance. Our job involves supporting and bearing witness, not putting our own personal beliefs onto those we care for. Even hospice chaplains are a neutral place of support, providing whatever the person or family needs. At the Hospice House, we are used to clergy members of a wide variety of religions visiting our patients. Very often, JJ will greet the visiting clergy in her usual charming manner. One day, I had an interesting interaction with a visitor when he discovered JJ belonged to me. "Can I ask you a personal question about the dog?" Certainly. "What is her spiritual background?" Um. "I'm Lutheran, does that count?" As the conversation continued, we did talk about how intuitive she can be and how she typically will seek those out who really need her. He was happy to pronounce this made her a deeply spiritual dog. This memory made me laugh later when I walked past a patient's room and glanced in to see JJ had joined a group of family members in a prayer circle around the bed. I learned later from one of the family members that JJ had arrived on her own, seemed to want to stay with them while they prayed, then when they finished, she left to continue her rounds. So, I've come to conclude that we now have our newest Hospice Chaplain. Who would have thought?

· · ·

JJ is an orally fixated Golden Retriever, as so many are. Her crate is stuffed to the gills with different kinds of toys that she will carry around from room to room. In JJ's *Handbook for Life*, it is written: "Thou shalt not greet people without a toy in your mouth," and she will look around in a panic trying to find one if someone is approaching her. She spends most days steadily emptying out her oversized toy box over our twelve-hour shift. Sometimes, she clings to a favorite for days, and other times it's a different toy each hour. Often, she will leave her toys behind in random rooms, almost as if it is her special calling card. Night shift has gotten used to finding them scattered throughout the building. JJ never was put through formal retriever training, as most of our other dogs have done, and she has developed her own style of interacting with people when she has a toy. I once saw a cartoon that had a dog with a ball saying: "No take. Throw. No take." JJ definitely believes in this philosophy. Visitors will think she wants them to take and throw her toy, but she has a different idea.

A cute, stuffed pink dragon—sans squeaker—is a recurring favorite for making rounds. It was the chosen one during the first Walkout JJ ever did with a toy in her mouth. It is not uncommon for people to bring a favorite stuffed animal from home and have it on their bed with them, especially those with memory issues. When we turn people in bed during our daily routine, we reposition the stuffed animal as well. One day, JJ spent time with a woman's family who had been visiting consistently. Some people experience a prolonged dying process over one, two, or even more weeks. It's what I call the "long goodbye," and it can be so exhausting for loved ones who want to be present at the bedside and yet still have lives to lead. This was one of those instances of a long goodbye and the family really enjoyed JJ's visits. One day, during this patient's stay, JJ brought Pink Dragon with her for a visit. The next morning, my CNA partner came out to show me a photo she just took of a patient and asked, "Isn't this JJ's Pink Dragon?" The toy was tucked under this woman's arms in a cuddle and had been with her all night. Apparently, the night shift didn't recognize it and kept it on the bed, repositioning them both every couple of hours. When I spoke with the patient's daughter, she said JJ had left it behind, so she'd put it up on the bed with her mom. The daughter was so pleased by the story and the photo of her mother getting the toy to cuddle, and told JJ: "It was like you kept her company all night long."

Many may remember my Pink Dragon. We were honored to be working on the day of this woman's death, and I had Pink Dragon on the floor as I snuggled with her granddaughter just before the Walkout.

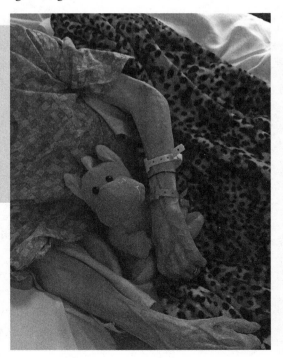

Since then we have found regular evidence of JJ checking in on patients by finding one of her toys placed on the bed. She doesn't get up on the beds without supervision, but will reach up to place a toy there. Each time it has been with people JJ visited more frequently, whether patient or family. This act of gifting her toys always makes family members smile and is usually mentioned in stories told to either the funeral director or our bereavement counselor.

"JJ, thanks for all of the love and support during this difficult time in our lives."

The gifts, however, might not entirely be acts of altruism. It is possible that in JJ's mind, she may feel dropping her toys off gives her some license to help herself to their items. When the Hospice House had only been open for a couple of months, we took care of a young man in his thirties. He came to us from a large teaching hospital in Portland and had many family members and friends visiting, including his five-month-old niece, who happened to be accompanied by a huge pink teddy bear. As I was doing some charting, I heard "JJ, no..." as the baby's father was following her down the hall. I could see she barely had a hold on the tip of the ear as she was clearly trying to make a sneaky exit.

Further, some of our volunteers make neck pillows for patients as they sit out front in the lobby waiting to greet visitors. Out of the blue, one day JJ decided she needed to help herself to one of the pillows. All I heard from the nurses' station was "JJ, no!" as she walked sheepishly back toward the nurses' station carrying it by the corner. Ultimately, it was decided that she needed her own personalized neck pillow, and she got to keep the one she had selected for herself. I am wondering if I need to change her name to JJ, No.

Each workday, JJ spends most of her naptime tucked under the desk in the nurses' station on a special blanket made for her by the wife of a patient who shared his meals with JJ. Often, it also is the area where she will gather her collection of toys for the day. Periodically, when the mood hits her, JJ decides to appoint herself the one to rehome patient and family slippers and socks. I shouldn't be surprised, as she is always carrying around my husband Tellus' socks or slippers at home. She is great at getting someone to give her some attention, and then ever so casually will pick up a slipper and walk out of the room with all the confidence of ownership in the world. When I don't catch her doing this, the item will usually end up in the pile of toys under the nurse's desk. I've never had anyone get mad over these antics—they tend to laugh at her behavior and enjoy the silly distraction that helps them forget for just a moment why we are all together.

Recently, one of the local funeral directors came into the Hospice House with a gift for JJ. It was one of the teddy bears that the staff gives out to young children of our patients. He was told the story of how one child spent time playing with JJ and the bear. I remember them well; I'd watch, as the youngster would offer the stuffed animal to JJ. While JJ would accept the bear into her mouth, getting it nice and sloppy wet as dogs do, she did not try to keep it. She seemed to know that it belonged to the child. As it happens sometimes, the patient died on a night shift, so the staff had packed up all the belongings—including the bear—and sent them to the funeral home for the family. But for some reason, when the family collected their things, they left the bear behind. The funeral director decided to bring the stuffed toy back for JJ to have, and this time she quickly added him to her collection. I removed his ribbon so that people recognize it is her bear.

• • •

Pain and anxiety at the end of life are treated with medicine, but distraction is another helpful tool, especially as we are waiting for the medication to take effect. JJ knows the commands "paws up," where she will put her paws wherever I direct her, and "snuggle" where she will get up on a bed with a person (which is possible because she's a petite Golden Retriever). If she can't be on the bed because there isn't room or the person is in pain, she can be in my lap next to the bed and in reach of the patient. This is where the distraction comes in: getting them to focus on an adorable dog can take their mind off what they are experiencing. JJ has also been helpful when someone is suspicious about and resistant to taking a medication. I have been amazed by the willingness of the person to take their medication simply because JJ was in my lap nearby when it was being administered. Mary Poppins may have been on to something when she sang, "just a spoonful of sugar makes the medicine go down." JJ is my sweet, secret weapon. She is a far less shady character than I am, especially when that person can snuggle with and pet her.

One gentleman was admitted to the Hospice House for agitation that could not be controlled at home. It was a bit of a struggle to try to keep him calm, so I thought maybe JJ would help. She did a "paws up" on the bed, and he settled once his hand reached her fur. However, the minute she would get back down, he would start up thrashing in the bed again. When someone is dying and has severe pain, agitation, or difficulty breathing, it creates a cascade of adrenaline in that person's body. Larger doses of medication will be needed more frequently to curtail this effect and allow the person to get comfortable. Since my patient had settled when JJ was near, I had her get up on the bed with him. As long as she stayed next to him, he rested quietly. It took thirty minutes before the medication took effect and JJ could get off the bed. In the meantime, she had a good nap while I finished charting on my work laptop as I sat next to them both.

JJ only does a bed visit when I am in the room to guide and supervise the interaction, and she will not stay on the bed if I leave the room. Audiences make her nervous, so she usually will only settle well during a bed visit when it's just the patient and us. JJ is not terribly fond of the Puparazzi whipping out their phones to snap photos of her, so I must be sneaky to get any pictures of her doing her special work. For patients who used to love dogs, we get frequent requests from their loved ones to have JJ do a bed visit, even if the person is not responding. This simple act provides a lot of comfort to their family members. When I say, "snuggle," it is more a matter of me giving JJ permission to do it, versus giving a command. JJ gets to decide if she will do it or not. I can read my dog's body language and know if it is a situation she is comfortable with, and I don't force her into an interaction she doesn't want to participate in. When she does indicate she would like to get up on a bed, it is important that I place her there, and very carefully, since so many people are experiencing pain or hypersensitivity or have very fragile skin that could tear. Families are touched by these special visits. One woman was especially thankful for the care given to her husband. Not only did JJ help eat his meals on an earlier admission, when he was close to dying, JJ got up on the bed with him and licked his hand. While his loss remains difficult, this wife has some wonderful memories of JJ, making her loss a bit easier.

Due to the nature of inpatient hospice work, JJ tends to spend far more time visiting family members and visitors rather than patients. While she is really not supposed to be up on furniture, on occasion she has snuggled with a family member on the couch in the patient's room. Inpatient hospice facilities are required to maintain a home-like environment, and there is nothing more home-like than having a dog around the Hospice

House. It is a common sight to look down the hall and see one or more people down on the floor with JJ, rubbing her belly and talking to her. It is an environment that helps the patient and the loved ones, and I can see it in the responses I get afterward. "Thank you, JJ, for just being there this last weekend. You helped me smile and hold it together more than you will ever know. My friend Johnnie passed shortly after I had to leave. I wish all hospitals and hospice were allowed to have animals. They are so good for the soul. Take care sweetie and big hugs to you and your crew for all you do."

• • •

JJ considers herself the official Meet and Greet staff member. She knows the door chime means someone is about to walk through the front door and she likes to keep track of our visitors. The first year we were open, she would get concerned about the groundskeepers walking by the windows and she would give us a warning bark. Since then, she has become accustomed to their weekly cleaning service and pays little attention to them. She rarely ever barks, but still will sound the alarm if someone comes through the first door and remains in the vestibule. In her mind apparently, only bad people hang out there. The lobby happens to be where JJ's cookie jar is located, and she has done her best to make sure all visitors, volunteers, and staff know exactly where that jar is with the teeny, tiny treats inside.

We have many family members who come to see our bereavement counselor once their loved one has died, but it can be hard for family members to come back to the building where their loved one passed. Seeing JJ dispels those feelings; she is a treat that brings smiles, not sadness. JJ likes these visits because most of them already know exactly where her cookie jar is. We've even had visitors who came to the building just to see JJ. One day she had to stay at home because of a hot spot on her skin that she kept scratching at. It was one of the few days I have ever been to work without her, and suddenly I heard her cookie jar rattle. Three times. The people I found in the lobby were incredibly disappointed to discover she was not working. I told them if they ever wanted to visit her, to just call and see what days we would be in.

Sometimes we have visitors to the building who aren't connected to any of our patients, but therapy dogs don't care why someone is visiting, they just want to meet them. JJ is no exception, playing hostess to those coming into her house and giving them love. Her affections and hugs are quite charming to people. No matter how sad someone is, JJ often can find a way to distract them and give them something to smile about. I remember one memorable note: "My Granny picked me up this morning from work. While waiting, our hospice therapy dog, JJ, provided her some comfort. It's been an especially hard year for our family. Granny has lost a niece and most recently a sister and a sister in law. Her only surviving brother is in poor health along with a brother in law. JJ sought her out intuitively knowing she needed her."

Many of the visitors to the Hospice House are children. JJ chooses which kids she wants to interact with, and I supervise the interaction to judge how safe the visit will be. JJ loves and is drawn to most children, but when we have especially boisterous kids around, she often will avoid them by spending time in the nurses' station. When I share stories about children visiting family members at the Hospice House, usually told through an interaction they had with JJ, people get very sad about the thought of children needing to deal with death. Some want to shield their children from the dying process, while others view it as a normal part of life. In hospice, we recognize the reality of needing to support families, including their children, so our team members are skilled at helping parents find a way to discuss this with their kids, including identifying the developmental stage that affects how a child deals with a death in the family. A three-year-old will have a very different experience than a young teenager. Yet, no matter what the age, most kids gravitate toward the support given by JJ. When families do bring their kids to the Hospice House, we are reminded how special it is to have several generations gathered together in support of one another. A child's laughter and smile remind us all about the circle of life.

One time we had several kids visiting their grandmother and they saw all of JJ's photo books and decided she must be famous. I had to spend some of the day "autographing" her calling cards with her paw print stamp. There was one boy JJ spent the most time with and after looking through the books, he asked me with a puzzled look on his face, "Why are you in this picture with JJ?" I did all I could to keep a straight face as I explained how I was connected to her. He decided then I needed to autograph JJ's card as well, but only the one for him, not the ones for his friends back home, for those he only wanted JJ's signature.

My people overheard something from the great-granddaughter of a patient as we were deep in conversation. "JJ, you have to come with me to Gigi's room, she's going to heaven and she needs your help." I did as she asked.

JJ is a help not just for the kids visiting, but for their guardians, who might need her to play a sort of a babysitter role while they focus on the loved one they are there to attend to. We often find JJ in the hallway, sharing her toys with kids or watching them play with Legos in the family room. As I made rounds one day, JJ was in a room with a young girl. Some visitors came into the room and asked JJ "So, who are you?" This young girl answered "This is JJ. She is my grandma's doctor." Our medical director happened to be in the room and he just laughed and nodded his head, agreeing with her. You often will hear him tell families "This dog has more degrees than most of us. She is a highly trained and qualified hospice dog and probably knows more than we do."

It does not happen often, but I will bring JJ in on my day off if there is a special need for a therapy dog. One family requested it for a young boy would be coming in the next day to say goodbye to his great-grandfather. This boy's grandparents were concerned he would have trouble as he was very close to the elderly man. As it turned out, like so many children before him, he had a good understanding for an eight-year-old and knew his "GG" was dying and spoke to me in a matter of fact and calm manner. Really, it was his father who was having the most difficult time and benefitted from JJ's attention.

When you have just turned eleven and it's time to say goodbye to your dad, a therapy dog can be one of the best comforts around.

We have some great community support for our Hospice House, especially by families whom we have served. One year, a local Girl Scout troop did a cookie drive for us. When the girls were selling cookies, people had the opportunity to buy additional boxes for our Hospice House family pantry. The first year, they collected sixty boxes of cookies for us, and we had both therapy dogs, JJ and Marfa, on hand for the delivery day. The girls and the troop leaders enjoyed spending time with the dogs, and the dogs loved the attention—and were certain the cookies were for them. It was a striking coincidence that this troop had selected the Hospice House as their project months before, because by the time of delivery day, JJ and I knew two of the girl scouts present as well as their mother who was a troop leader. We had been caring for their grandfather during that week at the Hospice House and he died later that day. The following year, they not only donated over two hundred boxes of cookies but boxes of other food for our family pantry as well. JJ was thrilled to see them all again, and I could tell the feeling was mutual.

When the Hospice House opened, we decided people's pets would be welcome to visit. Due to infection control concerns, we only allow in dogs and cats. We have guidelines in place, including keeping the door closed during a pet visit. JJ knows she doesn't get to visit most of the visiting pets, but she often is quite curious about the animals and will sniff at the closed door. When we have a cat visiting, they are typically happy not to have to see the therapy dog. Our one exception was when a Bengal cat was visiting and was on a harness and leash. JJ had followed me down the hall, walking past the room with the cat, watching him with mild curiosity. Until he suddenly let out a growl and hiss causing JJ to practically levitate sideways to get out of his way. She was then stuck at the end of the hall, with big eyes and a look that said "No way, crazy lady. I'm not walking past that tiger again." I had to close the door and give her much encouragement to head back to the nurses' station. It is an occasion I would have loved to have had on video.

We have far more dogs who visit the Hospice House than cats. Molly was one of the many dogs who have visited their people over the years. She was a very sweet girl and a great comfort to her dad at a very sad time when he was losing his wife. I am so glad our families have the option of pet visits here. It is a very bittersweet thing, for sure. It is clear pets know that things are changing and are not right with their people. While we as pet owners grieve for our animals' much shorter lives, our pets can grieve just as deeply when they are left behind, especially when they do not have a lot of animals around to distract them. When people suffer the loss of a loved one, very often their pets can help get them through their grieving process and vice versa.

I've never done this before, but BossyPants found me in a room staying with someone who was dying. Her people had gone home for a rest and left Molly's blanket on the couch. I'm not supposed to be on the furniture, but I figured I was a good stand-in for Molly and I got a pass. We stayed with her for her last breaths.

Since our outpatient staff is housed in the Hospice House, JJ spends a lot of time visiting different people throughout the day. While everyone knows they will get her attention when they have food, I frequently hear stories of how she has sought someone out who was having a difficult day. I'll get a note that says something like, "JJ has ignored me for the past two weeks, but today she just wouldn't leave my desk. I've been struggling with some things at home recently and I think she's picked up on it."

She has developed different relationships with those she sees on a routine basis, but it is clear she is especially fond of men. The first FedEx driver we had made sure to spoil her rotten; he kept cookies in his pocket ready for her and he always paused in his busy day to indulge her a quick hug. We've had many drivers for all kinds of deliveries since, and none of them quite understand why she sits next to them, staring at their pockets. If they leave without acknowledging her, she'll look so dejected that one of us will give her a cookie from her jar. She has trained one of her favorite patient transport drivers to give her belly rubs and cookies each time he is at the Hospice House, even if it is several times each day.

Our FedEx driver is THE BEST! I get wiggly when I see him. His pocket is always full of treats, and they have my name all over them. Sometimes I even get to go out to his truck to get more once he's emptied the cookie pocket.

JJ has a routine when we get to work. She must say hello to the night shift, and then sometimes she will join the CNAs giving report to snuggle them. JJ has several different collars hanging from her crate, each with a different bow or ribbon to let people know she's a girl. And because she is a girl, she cannot wear the same outfit two days in a row. Her Samaritan name badge hangs from her collar so everyone knows she is official. There have been a couple of times I have forgotten to put a collar on her and she will pull one off the crate and carry it around. Usually it is the collar from our previous work day that has her badge on it. Once the morning reports are finished, she is sure to say goodbye to everyone. One of our night nurses met JJ when she was just two days old and got to hold her. They have developed a ritual of lap snuggles with cookies once report is done and before she heads home for the day.

Throughout the course of a day, JJ will try to care for anyone who seems to need it. In our weekly hospice meetings, it is normal to have general announcements given before discussion of patient care, but one day, a staff member arrived with several kittens she had rescued from a patient's house to try to find them homes. Many of my co-workers had heard me tell stories of JJ's nanny skills with puppies, but everyone seemed surprised to see her checking out the kittens and even cleaning them. Her focus was on them and only them. She had no desire to leave the meeting when I did, and she spent the rest of the time staying next to them, making sure they were taken care of.

At this point, people all over our Samaritan Health Services system knew about JJ. There have been a few fun articles about her and her work shared on our internal computer network. Each time I was startled by this because I'd suddenly get random e-mails sent to me from people I did not know. I remember the first one read: "I LOVE your dog." Um, OK? It turned out that the article, "A Day in the Life of JJ," was on the front page of Samaritan's intranet. One of our local magazines featured this entertaining story about JJ's work at the Hospice House less than a year after we first opened. I suppose this was my glimpse into the way even a virtual therapy dog is helpful. I remember one message that said, "I wanted to tell you how much I enjoyed reading that little article about JJ. It brought tears to my eyes. When I was younger, more active, and outgoing I thought I wanted to be a nurse. When I was studying to become a CNA at a nursing facility, I learned that it takes a very special person to be able to see people through the end chapters of their lives. The work that you and JJ do is so important and touching. Thank you for bringing comfort to the people who built our community, drove our school buses, taught us, bagged our groceries, led our local governments, etc. You and JJ are making a difference so that a patient's final chapter doesn't have to be a sad one. Thank you for brightening my Saturday!"

As each year goes on, more people in the community have heard of or met JJ from her work at the Hospice House. Many of the thank you cards sent to the Hospice House will give a special thank you to her. She was even mentioned on a family satisfaction survey. In their answer to: "Was there anything that was most helpful?" The family member wrote: "JJ the dog. JJ was very warm and welcoming the days we saw her, just as she was when she helped my father-in-law last year. Thank you, JJ, for all you do for everyone during the end of life."

I have heard from staff members who have visitors or patients ask about JJ. Recently, I was very touched to receive this e-mail from a fellow hospice nurse: "I thought I would pass along a little kudos to JJ and TBO. Today, I went to drop off my kiddos before work and I just happened to be wearing scrubs. The childcare ladies asked me where I worked, and when I told them, their faces just lit up. 'Hey, do you know JJ?' 'Isn't she the best dog?' Both of them went on to relay how they had family members who had died here, and what a comfort they found her to be. One was really touched that JJ had come on her Walkout, and the other told how JJ went out first, sniffed the funeral home van 'to make sure it was good enough for my sister.' She also shared that during the worst of her grief, JJ came up and put her head on her leg and sat with her. Perhaps the highest compliment ever, 'JJ is the reason I got a dog of my own!' She got a service dog to help with her diabetes before having gastric bypass."

While many of the patients we care for at the Hospice House do die with us, there are many who come in just to have their symptoms stabilized so they can return home. JJ has been known to get up in the transport van with those whom she has bonded with to give some last love and support when they transfer home. We always wish them well and hope they have some very fine days ahead. For those who spent time enjoying JJ's company, I will tuck one of her calling cards in their belongings before they go home. While there are many patients who are not responsive, we do have some who can interact with JJ.

Sometimes, it's the very simple things that bring solace and peace. Enjoying fresh air and sunshine for the first time in a long while and petting a dog are two of these things. I got to help with both yesterday.

Since the Hospice House has opened, we have taken care of several spouses—some a year or two apart and some just a few months apart. Our hospice program has a big event each November called Light Up A Life. Every year we pay honor to those who have died during our hospice service. We have a slideshow with their names and photos, and their loved ones who can make it join us. Last year, we had 600 people and it was packed. Unfortunately, the list of the deceased gets longer each year. So far, it has been scheduled on my day off, and there are so many people who are happy to have the chance to see JJ again.

A few years back, one of these was a woman—I will call her Ann—whose husband died at the Hospice House the year before. She would delight in JJ's visits whenever visiting her husband. Afterward, when Ann started coming in for our hospice program's bereavement group, she would seek out JJ for a quick visit. At the Light Up A Life that year, she came up to talk to me afterward. Ann had recently been diagnosed with lung cancer and said, "When it's my time, I'm coming back to have you girls take care of me." She continued to visit anytime she came in for bereavement group, looking frailer each time, but she was able to maintain her spunky attitude. During one of these visits, Ann told me she would be signing into hospice and she knew she would eventually be coming in to have us take care of her. Six weeks later, on a Monday, we received the call that Ann was to be admitted to the Hospice House. She was rapidly declining, had symptoms out of control, and it was time. I was so thankful we were working that day. When she arrived, it was clear she would be with her husband again soon. Ann briefly recognized me, and her family recognized JJ from last year. JJ spent a lot of time comforting her loved ones as I worked on getting her symptoms controlled so she could have a peaceful death. For what it was, it was a good day doing what we do best.

Sometimes, just the antics of a dog bring smiles and comfort to those family members sitting vigil at the bedside. Visiting children can often get JJ to drop her toy at least once for them to throw it down the hallway. Her unique style of retrieving—waiting for a belly rub in exchange for the toy—is entertaining for people.

I have learned to take my cues from JJ and follow her lead. Normally, she knows when the day is winding down and is ready to go home and have her dinner, but there have been times when my shift is over and she clearly feels she has work still to do. One evening after report, she wasn't in the nurses' station waiting for me, and I had to go room to room in search of her. When I found her, JJ was hugging a sobbing woman at the bedside of her dying father. I quietly left the room, clocked out, and waited. About ten minutes later, JJ came trotting down the hall, finally ready to head home.

• • •

One of the common things people do at the end of their lives is called life review. This is the term used when people reminisce about their life history through memories, stories, and reflection and it helps give meaning to their own lives along the way. We had one woman who adored dogs and spent a lot of time with JJ, even learning her snuggle command. I recall I had a nursing student shadowing me, learning the essence of hospice care even down to the value JJ brought. The student watched as I asked simple questions in an effort to get the woman to tell the stories she wanted to share, while the woman was aided by cuddles with JJ. The focus in hospice work is very different for nursing students to see in comparison to their time in the hospital. Hospice focuses on the big picture, and since we all are very much aware about how time is limited for those we care for, it is easy for us to focus on the essentials at the end of life. Along with assessing physical symptoms, emotional and spiritual matters are just as—and even more so at times—important. JJ often can help draw out stories as patients and/or families reflect back over time. When we have nursing students follow us for the day, we can talk with them about the things that are important for patients when they are at the end of their lives. And, in addition, a hospice rotation can be stressful for students who have never dealt with any kind of death. Many have discovered JJ will comfort them as well.

I had a special bed visit to do, and not only did I get some pets, but somehow this very special lady named Carol found the strength to give me a hug. I am sorry that it made her people cry a bit. I know it was a bittersweet time for them, as she only had the energy to rouse briefly. She has cancer, and she wrapped her thin arms around me, happy to have a dog to snuggle with her again. These brief moments make time stand still, if only for a fleeting minute, for those whose time to say goodbye is drawing very near. I know Carol's two greyhounds, along with a multitude of loved ones, are waiting for her on the other side.

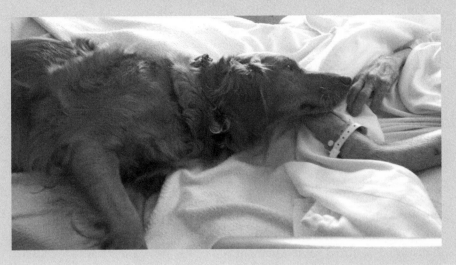

When I shared this story online, it was touching to Carol's family members who witnessed this memorable scene at the Hospice House earlier that month. Some of them followed JJ's page and shared photos. "Imagine my surprise coming to your page today, JJ, and seeing such a beautiful photograph and story about you and my mama. Thank you, thank you, thank you JJ and scribe, for joining hands with God to give us a very special bon voyage." These are the words that help keep the passion for our work. "How lovely of your scribe to tell this story. JJ, you were such a big part of our journey at hospice." However, that was just the beginning of this very special story. Carol's daughter told me why she had gotten so teary the first day we took care of her mom, when she first saw JJ follow me into their room. When Carol was diagnosed with her cancer, her daughter asked her to promise she would find a way to visit her once she was gone. They decided it would be best through a dog, since they all loved dogs. After some research, they both decided that she was most like a Golden Retriever and thus, her visits and messages would be through a Golden. Her daughter just about lost it when JJ walked into the room that day. "God works in mysterious and amazing ways."

One of the reasons I limit JJ's availability for extra volunteer visits and crisis response callouts is because sometimes our workday can be on the scale of a crisis callout with intense emotion all around. Hospice services are available for those who have a prognosis of six months, though, quite often, we deal with people who only have hours or days. At times, there just is so little time to prepare for a loved one's death, and it all seems to go at the speed of light. It is a time that can feel a little traumatic for families and even staff.

When a person has been hospitalized with every treatment possible attempted, it is often difficult for family members and the medical team to come to grips when these treatments become futile. Very often the person is close to death when they transition to comfort care, but families often either are not told or don't hear this frank assessment. Hospice workers are skilled at the often subtle assessments that indicate when someone is on the verge of dying, so once the person arrives with us, it is one of the most challenging conversations we need to have with their family members, especially when we can tell right away there may only be a few hours left. It is our job to prepare everyone for what is happening, even when people aren't ready to hear this news. These are the times JJ often will step in to provide some comfort and distraction, and she keeps herself busy passing out hugs to everyone. While we must say the things we do, it's hard for anyone to absorb what is being said—but it's not hard to accept the comfort and love of a dog during these sad times. And JJ always seems to know exactly who needs her most. One message I received illustrated exactly how JJ helps: "I wish I lived closer because I would love to tell how precious you are, JJ. I'm not a dog person, but you didn't let that stop you when you knew I needed you. You just marched in and snuggled with me and let me hug you and cry. You are special."

6

One of the most common questions I get is if JJ feels sadness or if she gets melancholy being around so much death and dying. Some of this, I am sure, comes from the emotional weight visible in the photos and stories I've shared of such intimate stories of the end of life—a snapshot in time, if you will, during a very sad time. As one woman told me, "Your most powerful posts evoke a visceral response." Most of the public remains afraid or in denial of death. Those of us who do hospice and palliative care work are comfortable bearing witness and being quietly present at the end of someone's life. We specialize in guiding people and their loved ones though a physical, emotional, and spiritual journey that all of us one day will go through, barring unexpected, sudden death. It's our job to normalize the process of dying and to take some of the mystery out of it, so people can prepare and focus on the person who will soon be gone.

JJ's job is different. When she's not snoring away under the counter in the nurses' station, she's there to be a comfort, a silly distraction, a playful babysitter, and a supporter. She doesn't experience the same emotional process that the humans are going through. Because of people's fear or anxiety about death, they often end up projecting those fears onto JJ. In our dog-happy culture, it is easy to attribute human emotion onto our animals, something called anthropomorphizing. While dogs express the simpler emotions, equivalent to a young child, they don't grasp the concept of the permanence of death. When I show a photo of a Walkout or of JJ hugging a family member, it's easy to think she is deeply affected, because people can imagine how hard it would be for them in that moment. But if you asked staff members who know JJ well, they would tell you about the myriad ways she easily shakes off any of the intense emotions around her. After a Walkout, she will run laps in the field, play with one of her toys, or, quite literally, come back into the building and give herself a good shake. I would expect her to be aware and even depressed if it were my husband or I that died and left her behind. Dogs who have experienced loss in their households will wait and wait for the person or pet sibling to return.

I also know of therapy dog handlers who make rounds to facilities month after month, so the dogs get to know the residents over time. When a facility resident dies, those therapy dogs that have established a relationship with that person over time, might show signs of sadness and depression when entering the room and expecting to find the person they know. But at the Hospice House, we have a very rapid turnover, and JJ often spends more time with families than with patients.

What will affect JJ is the sheer number of emotional and stressed people she deals with. It doesn't happen very often, but sometimes we have large families visiting at the same time. It can be very tiring for her to visit with so many people, especially when there are a lot of kids. She will show signs, usually displaying immense fatigue, when she has been dealing with those who have intense emotions. But she gets to choose whom she interacts with, and it is my job to look out for her and enforce when she tells me she needs a break. She is very intuitive and on occasion, has not wanted to interact with someone. I trust her judgment and will make some excuse about her needing to take a break or go outside.

It's important for her to rest whenever she wants to, so when she is soundly sleeping we avoid waking her up. We know that if she gets into her crate, it means she really needs a timeout. This action—JJ crating herself—happens in waves. Sometimes she will go months without going in for anything other than to fish out another toy. Her crate in the nurses' station is a giant toy box for the most part, and she will dig and send toys flying when she really wants to sleep uninterrupted. She uses it so infrequently that when she disappears, I will search the whole building before I think to check her crate. At that point, she'll give me a look with a half open eye as if to say, "You really weren't the pick of the litter, were you?"

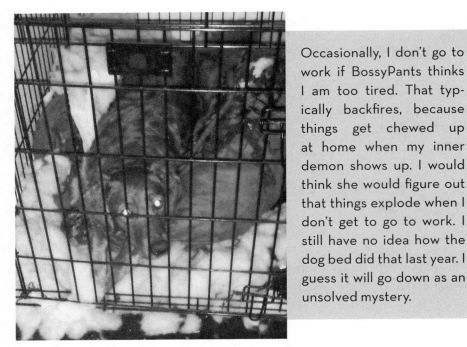

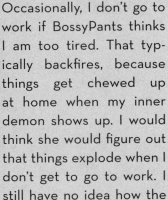

Occasionally, I don't go to work if BossyPants thinks I am too tired. That typically backfires, because things get chewed up at home when my inner demon shows up. I would think she would figure out that things explode when I don't get to go to work. I still have no idea how the dog bed did that last year. I guess it will go down as an unsolved mystery.

As any handler of a therapy or crisis response dog should be doing, my most important job is to ensure JJ doesn't get worked too hard. This is especially important in relation to the different jobs she has. I am the one who signed her up for this, so it falls on me to make certain that she still wants to visit with people, that she feels safe and protected, and that she is not forced to do something she doesn't want to. Now that therapy animals— dogs especially—are becoming more popular, discussions are occurring about the welfare of these animals. Their needs must come first, handlers must recognize when a dog needs a break, must find ways to decrease their stress, and make sure the animal has a way to relax and have fun. JJ and I have long stretches of time off, during which JJ gets to play, sleep, and live the life of being "just a dog."

As one of our Project Canine board members pointed out, "Perhaps the most surprising part of the worldwide phenomenon of JJ's video is the concern that seems to keep coming up about her welfare. I guess it's surprising because we know how well you take care of her and how truly happy and fulfilled she is. There are few, if any, dogs on this planet whose lives are better than hers." Because I didn't want JJ to burn out, I brought Gamine out of retirement at the age of twelve to help with the volunteer visits. She had been retired for a few years, but clearly still loved to visit with people. Because of the hospice work we do, I have chosen to limit JJ's availability for both local volunteer therapy dog visits as well as callouts with Hope Animal-Assisted Crisis Response. During one intense month at the Hospice House, we had patients in their thirties, forties, and fifties, with several Walkouts many of those days. That month at work felt very crisis oriented for both JJ and me, and we would go home exhausted. Because of this, when I was asked to deploy with HOPE to Washington State after a school shooting, I chose to stay home.

Compassion fatigue is a term that has been talked about a lot in the media recently. It often is seen in veterinary medicine, animal rescue work, and in different areas of medicine and nursing. Compassion fatigue is defined as loss of satisfaction that comes from doing one's job well, or job-related distress that outweighs job satisfaction. Sometimes, merely being exposed to another's traumatic experience can leave people feeling emotionally distraught. In nursing, it is common for us to talk about self-care as a balance for this, but we are not necessarily the best at putting it into practice. Self-care involves the actions a person takes to care for their physical, mental, and emotional health. This can be a challenge for many people, especially those in health care who are used to caring for others, not themselves. Compassion fatigue is big in hospice, especially for those who have difficulty in maintaining boundaries. We acknowledge and support the sadness and grieving of families, but it is not our job to take it on. People don't last long in end-of-life care if they cannot find a way to leave work behind or if they become drawn in and overwhelmed by the sadness hospice families experience.

JJ is the queen of self-care. I take notes from watching her—when she walks away from an interaction with a grieving family member and simply shakes it off, I am reminded to do my own little head and shoulder roll and take some deep breaths and relax. It's amazing how effective this can be during a workday. Humans could learn a thing or two about coping with stressors by following her lead. As someone once pointed out on JJ's page, "Dogs are so good at being able to remind us all of how healing it is for the caregivers to be able to let go and play." It has helped me take care of myself when I am aware that JJ needs attention and time off. Nurses are tough nuts to crack, but give me a dog to focus on and I'll make sure she is taken care of. When she plays, it helps me to unwind by watching and playing with her. As with all dogs, JJ lives in the moment, another thing that is a helpful reminder regarding my hospice work. Dogs are so good at being able to remind us all how healing it is for caregivers to let go and play. In addition to digging for gophers and swimming nonstop, JJ has a multitude of dog friends at home to chase and play with. Since I must be outside to supervise, I can only enjoy those occasions and delight in their antics. Having fun keeps JJ's batteries charged and mine too, for the most part.

"Let's run in the field," they said. "Good exercise," they said. "Need to clean off," I said, as I jumped into a very mucky deep puddle hearing "NOOOOOOOOOOOO" behind me. I then helped the woman out by going swimming in a less muddy deep pool. I offered to comfort her and was promptly turned down.

It's always an adventure living with so many dogs. It leaves me either feeling young or like I'm about to pull my hair out, but it always makes me laugh, even if the laughter occurs a little after the fact. No matter what wonderful jobs our dogs have, at the end of the day they are still just dogs, even JJ. When I left her in the house one day while I ran to the Hospice House for a therapy dog shadow visit with a new team, I was in a hurry and had not checked the house thoroughly before leaving. When I returned, JJ was hiding in the bedroom waiting for me to discover the artwork she created with a full bag of garbage left out in the kitchen. People seem relieved to hear of the naughty antics of a stellar therapy dog, making her just a regular dog, while personally, I wish I was better at paying attention to prevent such mischief.

Many Golden owners know exactly how much their dogs love to roll in things, the smellier the better. While we built our house, we were living temporarily on 600 acres in a small trailer. There were plenty of animals around, including elk, and one afternoon I heard Tellus grumbling, "Why do the dang Goldens have to find the smelliest thing to roll in?" A few minutes later I collapsed laughing because one of the Labs did the very same thing. We had fourteen dogs running and playing, with Goldie, the Lakeland Terrier, running behind barking her bossy orders at the bigger dogs. If it is outside, the shenanigans are just funny—we put the outdoor shower to use frequently.

Along with playtime on our days off, I also started taking JJ to activities that don't focus on humans and their emotions, one of which was a class on Nose Work. Nose Work is a fun search and scenting activity that keeps dogs physically and mentally fit. It involved JJ using her nose to find treats hidden in boxes so, to no one's surprise, she enjoyed the games immensely. And I find that taking classes not only gives her something fun to do, it helps to enrich her life and build on our relationship.

When I heard about Barn Hunting, I thought it might be just the thing for JJ, possibly more so than Nose Work. Barn Hunting is an event where dogs hunt for a rat in a straw maze. I didn't know much about the details, so I brought JJ to an introductory workshop, where her Dalmatian boyfriend Casey was participating. I was cautiously skeptical, as I really wasn't sure how any of it worked or what happened to the rats, but the workshop instructor described how the rats used in Barn Hunt are typically family pets, raised around dogs. She had several that lived very happily with her own dogs. The Barn Hunting Association describes how the rats are comfortable in their safe, aerated tubes and are picked because they enjoy interacting with the dogs. When JJ was first introduced to the rat, he was safely tucked away in a wire mesh cage. I was amazed to see how calm and curious he was with the dogs. JJ, on the other hand, was not what I would call calm, but was laser focused on this delightful, friendly find and wore her "cowabunga, dude!" expression. The rats are kept in their ventilated PVC tubes on the course and their safety is of utmost importance. It turns out the rats have a great union, so they get plenty of breaks. There is even a position called the Rat Wrangler, whose primary job at events is to make sure the rats are safe and cared for. At the workshop, we were coached on how to properly pick up the tube horizontally so the rat couldn't get hurt. After this, I was very comfortable with the idea of trying out this event with JJ, especially since I didn't have to touch the rat.

As with most dog events, there are different classes of difficulty. In the beginner, or novice, level, three tubes are placed on the course. One is empty, one holds dirty rat litter from a cage, and the third has the rat. The dog's job is to find which tube has the little Templeton and indicate this to his or her handler, who then calls "rat." It's a test of both the dog's hunting and scenting abilities, but also the partnership between dog and human since the handler has to read the dog's signals correctly. During the workshop, JJ clearly loved the game and was fast at finding the correct tube. When I was watching other dogs, I could see how determining which tube was the correct one could be difficult. Some dogs froze, some seemed to give little hint to their handler, and then there was JJ. She would nose the tube around the straw and then nibble on the end. It was very easy for me to recognize her behavior and call "rat." There are two other components of the Barn Hunt that the dogs need to complete to qualify. The first is to climb on the straw bale at least once and the second requires the dog to go through a tunnel built into the straw course. If the dog successfully meets all the required elements, it is considered a qualification pass that counts toward the title at that level.

After the workshop, I decided to enter JJ in a Barn Hunt. When I tried to introduce her to the tunneling, I think she thought I was a bit nuts and this portion ultimately took a lot of practice on our part. We worked the week between the workshop and the Barn Hunt, so on one slow day, I used break time to practice with some makeshift tunnels built from flattened cardboard boxes and chairs. I'm quite certain JJ thought I had lost my mind, but treats were involved, so she went along with my crazy idea. My co-workers just shook their heads at me, but it worked and she got the idea of what the "tunnel" command meant. Tellus already had several large round bales and smaller straw ones delivered to our new property to break up the flat field when training the retrievers. When I stopped by with JJ, she thought she had hit the jackpot and made a beeline for the straw. To this day, she and her sister Ottie spend a lot of time hunting the bales. I truly hope she doesn't catch something since it won't be safely stashed in a tube.

We spent the weekend at our first Barn Hunting event playing in the straw, hunting down an elusive Templeton, and hanging out with Casey and his owner. I hadn't really noticed how slippery the straw was when we were at the workshop. They had only had a few bales set up, and the ground wasn't thoroughly covered in straw like it is at an actual Barn Hunt. Our first day was a success, with two qualifications and a first place for the fastest time in her class of large dogs. We went home with three ribbons that day. Tellus hadn't been able to come out and watch, so he made it the next day to see what all the fuss was about. I didn't know at the time, but he took video of our last run when JJ earned another qualification ribbon and completed her novice title. Being the graceful handler that I am, as I walked back toward the tunnel after she found the rat, I upended and landed squarely on my bottom, bouncing right back onto my feet as if nothing had ever happened. Did I mention that straw is slippery? We still laugh about this, since Tellus swears I trip on the air around me. We have discussed setting up a straw course on our property and acquiring some pet rats, but…rats. I tried to bargain with Casey's mom saying we would have the course set up on our property if she would keep the rats at her house. We still are in negotiations. JJ may be out of luck on advancing to the upper levels of Barn Hunt unless I get extremely motivated.

Many people can fully relax and unwind once they are at home, and JJ is no exception. She has her therapy person, my husband, and her therapy cat, Taz, to relax her. She's become a bit like Jekyll and Hyde in her personalities. She is extremely calm and laid back at work, resting up for when it's time to come home. Once she's back home, she goes nuts when she sees Tellus, does wind sprints in the field, and if we had a pond again, she would be swimming constantly. She is very spoiled at work and at home. Her favorite time is when Tellus gives her the "snuggle" command and she jumps up in his lap. She practically purrs like a cat, smiling and closing her eyes in bliss. If she had her way, she would stay there all evening long.

Luckily, there's always popcorn before bed. When I get home, my kitten and I wrestle and play for about ten minutes. He's a bit piggish when it comes to popcorn. The zookeepers just keep shaking their heads around here. Our philosophy: Keep 'em guessing. They might just be too confused to realize how many treats we are getting.

JJ has made many trips to Montana and is just as enamored of the place as Callie was. At my parents' house in Whitefish, she was quick to resume the squirrel watch, protecting us all from the dangerous creatures. When we go on our road trips, I make frequent stops to stretch my legs and let the dogs take a break. One of my favorite places to do this in Montana is along an area from St. Regis to the Flathead Valley. Since I was eighteen and going to college in Tacoma, Washington, I have made the drive countless times along this route. The Clark Fork River winds along the highway and I always have made it one of my stopping places, especially once I had dogs. Callie, Gamine, Dash, JJ, and Ottie have all taken a swim and stretched their legs here. It is always in this place where JJ practices her own style of Montana Barn Hunting. After taking a swim, she'll go into hunting mode. One time, she had clearly smelled a critter and tracked the scent under a large log. When I think back on it, this was a terrible idea. At home, the most she will stumble on might be a small rodent or a young possum, but in Montana, there are all sorts of animals, including badgers, weasels, and skunks, which might be hiding under a log. Thankfully, it was nothing but the old scent, and I am a bit more cautious of where I let her explore now.

Montana is a great place to get antlers! Though Ms. CrankyPants got upset when I jumped the fence. Ha! What would you expect with a 2-foot-high "fence?" Woman, you have taught me to jump higher than that. I was simply going to follow the deer trail at the house and find some more antlers. I could sell them and buy my own BACON!

One of the downsides of JJ being able to roam free most days at work is the number of treats she gets. The size of her dinner each day is in direct proportion to the amounts of treats I know she has received, no matter how hard she tries to convince me otherwise. At home, it doesn't help that Tellus is a sucker for the dogs in their quest for the never-ending snack. They have learned to keep their eye on him, because he will usually fold. Several years ago, on one of his trips running competitions, he found something called bacon jerky and brought it home. Not only was he in heaven, but the dogs were too once they got a bite. To say those in my household prefer super healthy fare would be patently untrue.

Doing some shopping at our favorite store and passing out hugs. I even got a fish skin treat. COWABUNGA! Bah-HumBugPants is not impressed with my breath now and says it's a good thing it's a day off. Hmmppphhhh.

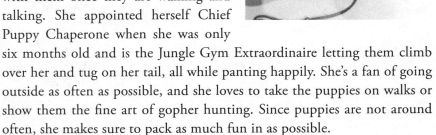

As much as I love having puppies around, I think JJ may have me beat in that category. She loves being with them from day one, although really seems to enjoy spending time with them once they are walking and talking. She appointed herself Chief Puppy Chaperone when she was only six months old and is the Jungle Gym Extraordinaire letting them climb over her and tug on her tail, all while panting happily. She's a fan of going outside as often as possible, and she loves to take the puppies on walks or show them the fine art of gopher hunting. Since puppies are not around often, she makes sure to pack as much fun in as possible.

While she may make me crazy at times, JJ continues to teach me the value of enjoying each day, shaking off the things that bother me, and experiencing the world with complete joy and an adventurous spirit. Her abiding message is: Live graciously, love fully and treasure the world around you.

7

When my husband, Tellus, and I first got together in 2004, he was asked by someone to whelp a litter of Goldens. He had been training dogs and had raised many litters for years before we had even met, because—for different reasons, such as health problems or not having time to raise a litter—some breeders ask others to raise a litter of puppies for them. In the case of the Golden due to have puppies, the owner was having some health issues. This litter was my first introduction to whelping, and I found it was a good balance to the end of life nursing care I perform. We received three puppies for our service and ended up keeping a male named Cowboy, while one of the females went to friends of ours in Oregon. Before this female puppy turned two, we got a phone call asking if we wanted to take her back—they were experiencing health problems and couldn't manage care of the dog. I didn't know it at the time, but my first "heart dog" had come back home to us. A heart dog is how I describe that once in a lifetime, soul mate dog, where the level of communication and bonding you have is deeper than any you had with other dogs. I do believe you can have more than one, and luckily, I have one in JJ, although I call her my heart and soul dog. Callie came back to us the year before we moved to Oregon, and we gave her the registered name of Calhoun's Wanna Be A Cowgirl.

Callie was sweet and fun to have around. She was my shadow from the start and a bit of a princess. We chose not to do formal field training with her since she was intended just to be a companion for me. She and Dash had their own puppies, twelve in all, while we were still in California. She was a fantastic mother, though when the puppies were born, my husband and I were both thrown off by one little girl who had a big black patch over one eye. We had never seen such a thing, and we wondered, "Did one of the black Labs get to her?" Our vet laughed and said if that were to have happened, she would be black all over. No, it was just a birthmark. We nicknamed her Patches, and because of her unique marking I probably held her at least twice as often as the other puppies when they were young. When it was time to go home to families, the children tended to love her, while the parents were not keen on her black patch. I had warned the final family who would be getting a puppy that they could end up with this mismarked dog. It turned out they had secretly hoped she would be theirs, so she was officially named Stormy and went to live a great life with them.

Callie was a natural mother and did a great job with her own puppies, but she adored any baby creature, which we learned earlier when we had a Labrador mother who was not the fondest of cleaning up her one and only litter. The mother dog made it clear she thought cleanup duty was beneath her, but I simply couldn't keep them clean enough by myself. Callie had wanted in with the litter the moment she knew they had arrived, so we decided to give her a chance and started putting her in with the puppies several times a day when their mother was out taking a break. Callie was thrilled with the nanny job, and we were amazed by her attentiveness to cleaning and tending puppies that were not hers.

Once we made the move to Oregon in 2007, I decided to pursue getting Callie into therapy dog work since she showed such an aptitude for it. She easily passed the test her first time and charmed the evaluator in the process. She joined Marfa, a black Lab mix, at hospice providing love to staff, patients, and families. At the time, we only saw patients in private homes or in a variety of facilities, such as nursing homes and assisted living communities, as the Hospice House had not yet been built. Callie would work with me most days unless the weather was too hot to safely take her along. She was the first dog I had ever had accompany me to work, and I learned many lessons along the way.

Marfa's owner, Anne, and I were always very careful to screen the private homes we went into. If there were other pets living in the home, or if it was not a safe environment, we did not bring our dogs in for a visit. I remember taking care of one gentleman in his late thirties who had cancer.

He had gone back to live with his parents while on hospice, and Callie's visits were a blessing to all. While the parents wanted guidance from me regarding their son's care, they also really enjoyed spending time with Callie and even bought her a special tub of biscuits. Callie was no different than JJ is now in the mooching department, and she hit the mother lode at that house. I couldn't say no—giving Callie a biscuit and spending time petting her was clearly getting them through the day. And Callie had a good memory. It took only one visit for her to recall where those biscuits were kept, which made her benefactors laugh even more. While all our hospice team members do a fantastic job at giving support, there is just something about the unconditional love a dog brings that none of us could provide for this family.

When I would take Callie to visit hospice patients at facilities, it absolutely made the day of most everyone who worked there. From patients to staff to families, having a few minutes to pet a dog was a mood lifter. Because there were so many people in the facilities, we would interact with many who were not our hospice patients or families. I always knew to schedule a bit more time when I went into one of these facilities with Callie. Once I started visiting memory care facilities with her, I quickly learned how therapy dogs often triggered memories from childhood for these residents. Time and time again she was referred to as "Fred" or "Ginger" from a past lifetime and I learned to just roll with it. Often it was the one and only way for them to connect with someone lost in the past. There were many sweet occasions where the resident would share stories from their childhood because of this very special dog who seemed to be able to connect with anyone she met. Because the staff of some of these facilities recognized the benefits that came from Callie's visits, I was later allowed to bring JJ in as a puppy to work on her socialization and training in preparation for her therapy dog evaluation.

As home hospice nurses, we are assigned our own set of patients to manage and care for. My area overlapped another nurse's, Catherine, so we frequently would cover vacations and time off for one another. My nurse partner Catherine had one patient by the name of Nora on service for many months, so I got to see her frequently during Catherine's off days, which was great since Nora loved dogs. She was an absolute hoot and her spunk reminded me so much of my own Greek grandmother, who had died some years earlier. Nora enjoyed life and was the embodiment of *joie de vivre*, although she would not have appreciated such a fancy term applied to her. Years later, I just I can't help smiling when I think of her. On our first visit, Nora gave Callie a small, white beanie toy dog from a collection she had. At the end of our visit, Callie watched her put it back in a large basket with the other toys. From then on, whenever we visited, Callie would make a beeline to the basket to get her toy, no matter how long it had been since we had last visited. It gave Nora great joy to watch Callie pick out the right toy and come prancing toward her, shaking it around. Callie was never one to destroy toys, so her beanie had some slobber, but was none the worse for wear. Nora told all the hospice team members about it any chance she could get. Most of my visits were spent talking about and interacting with Callie, and I had to sneak in my nursing work. Shortly before Nora died, she gave Callie the little beanie dog to take home.

Callie showing off her beanie dog at Nora's home during one of her hospice visits.

While we spent time with patients, families, and facility staff, probably half of Callie's time was spent giving hospice staff love and comfort. Caring for those who are terminally ill, whether directly or indirectly, can be quite stressful. It was common for all my co-workers to spend time with Callie at some point. She was helpful in keeping the mood light when she was around and she was known for her incredible mooching skills. As one person remembers: "She was so full of love and quick to offer it to all. And of course, she loved her treats. I fell in love with her the first time I met her! She always brought a smile to my face and joy to my heart when she was in the office."

Each week, all hospice programs are required to participate in something called Interdisciplinary Team meetings, also known as IDT. It's a time when all the hospice team members come together to provide important insights that contribute to the care of our patient and families. Callie would roam the packed conference room, spending time with whomever she felt she needed to see. As one colleague reports: "She was my introduction to therapy dogs. I loved sitting in the back of the conference room and feeling her love during IDT. I do believe the atmosphere of the meeting was tempered by the presence of Callie and Marfa." Callie also had the art of begging down to a science and more than one sandwich stashed in a bag on the floor disappeared before people realized they needed to put lunches out of reach. She came from hunting dog lines and knew how to use her nose. As a nurse who is now our hospice manager recalls, "I remember her 'sharing' people's food, without permission!"

Callie became my personal therapy dog the year my mother was diagnosed with Amyotrophic Lateral Sclerosis, or ALS. Because there are no clinics in Montana that specialize in ALS, we were given the option to travel to Minnesota, Utah, or Washington to confirm her possible diagnosis by her local neurologist. We chose Seattle since it was easy for me to get around. I had lived so many years there and knew the area and hospitals. Mom was admitted to the local hospice program in Montana shortly after the definitive ALS diagnosis in Seattle. As an experienced hospice nurse, I knew how this would go. ALS is always fatal, and it was very clear by how rapidly Mom was declining that her time would be short. Callie made most of the trips with me every few weeks from Oregon back home to Montana, keeping me company on the twelve-hour drives back and forth to Whitefish. She also was a great comfort to both of my parents, though their Miniature Schnauzer, Jazz, didn't know what to make of the intruder. True to her nature, Callie found a way to calm Jazz and show she wasn't a threat.

When my mom ended up moving into a facility due to her high-care needs, we would make our visits there. It was common during those times to have people seek Callie out for a quick visit. Not only was she good for my parents, having her around for me was a great distraction. She needed to be taken care of and get exercise too, and taking her for a swim or a hike gave me some much-needed downtime. She made me laugh, which is very beneficial when someone so close to you is dying. Callie loved Montana and fancied herself a great hunter. My parents' house was like a wildlife safari on a forested lot. She was overwhelmed choosing whether to stalk the deer, turkeys, squirrels, chipmunks, or birds. Oh, the tough decisions for a dog. Luckily, we were spared any bear or mountain lion visits, though it was not uncommon for a bear or its cubs to end up near the deck of my parents' house, attracted by the abundance of sunflower seeds that my parents put out to feed the birds, squirrels, and deer. My dad had built a dog kennel when we first moved into the house in the 1970s, which later sat unused just off the back deck. Several years ago, a cub got into the kennel and couldn't get out. He screamed his head off and had Mama Bear making a racket. My parents were trying to figure out what to do and were preparing to call Fish and Game when eventually, the cub found his way out. So knowing the possibilities of big predators in the area, I was happy that my visits with Callie were uneventful, with her declaring her nemeses only the chipmunks and squirrels.

During one of our later visits to my mom, Callie was pregnant. At one of our frequent fuel stops on the drive out, I got a mushroom burger for the road, but bought it before popping in for a bathroom break and left it in the car. When I came back, all I could see was Callie smiling and licking her lips, not a burger in sight. She wasn't the least bit remorseful, her expression said: "What? I'm growing puppies. Cut me some slack." Back to the burger joint I went for a replacement swearing, "Really, the dog ate it!" as they laughed at me. People would stare at Callie, as her pregnant belly was quite huge by then, but it didn't slow her down one bit. She was too busy having the time of her life. When she wasn't with Mom giving some love, she continued her war with the squirrels. We did have one close call with her at the house as I was preparing to drive back west. I had scanned the area before letting her out on the back deck, then watched as she cruised over to the squirrel area for a bit of a chase. Almost immediately, I saw a black and white tail go straight up in the air, and I ran out yelling like a banshee. Fortunately, I scared the skunk away before it could spray her. That would not have made for a pleasant ride home.

Two weeks after we returned home, Callie delivered twelve healthy puppies without a fuss. I often say I get to be a midwife at the end of the life cycle and on occasion, at the beginning, however, my work has never been so personal. As my mom was getting close to her final goodbye, there was something so bittersweet about welcoming this group of puppies into the world. We don't typically name our litters, but this one was quickly designated, "Mom's Litter." During our last trip, Mom had been eager to know how Callie would do with the puppies. I had promised to let her know once they arrived. When I called the next day to share the news, it was clear she was declining quickly because she had to have someone hold the phone to her ear. I am told she managed a smile, even though she was no longer able to talk. I was in frequent contact with her hospice nurse, and planned to fly back to Montana in a few days once my husband returned home from a road trip. Then I got a phone call at the end of the workday, "Come now if you want to be here." Thanks to so many, including my husband who raced home to Callie and her new brood, I made it in time.

Callie with "Mom's Litter" giving love and comfort in Montana.

When it came time for a memorial service a couple of weeks later, there was no question that my husband and I would both be there. We didn't have anyone we could trust with the puppies, but Callie was a trooper, so we loaded up with her twelve, two-and-a-half-week-old puppies and hit the road. Mom would have absolutely loved it. We had always been adventurous, but this was one of our biggest adventures ever. Our truck happened to have a specially made dog box that allowed us to carry up to sixteen adult dogs. This let us travel with the rest of our dogs without having to scramble to find someone last minute to take care of them. Luckily it also had an extended cab, so every two hours we would rotate six puppies to nurse and be cleaned, while I sat in the back with them. The other six puppies slept in a warming basket on the front seat. Once we made it to Montana, we set up a temporary pen and as usual, Callie was not worried in the least so long as she had her puppies nearby to keep an eye on them.

Callie and the puppies were a great stress reliever for our family during this very sad time. Our two nephews got to hold the puppies and play with Callie and we were all reminded of the circle of life. Callie had been there for me during Mom's illness, just as she and "Mom's Litter" were there for our whole human family. Also at this time, Gamine was pregnant with JJ and her littermates. Since Callie and Gamine were both getting older, and I needed to have at least one puppy to have as a future potential therapy dog, we planned to keep one from each litter.

Gamine had her puppies six weeks after Callie had "Mom's Litter." While Callie's puppies would still occasionally nurse recreationally, by that time they were very happy to eat their puppy food. Gamine and Callie are unusual mother dogs in that they have the philosophy "it takes a village" when it came to raising puppies—it was common to find both moms in the whelping box, helping each other out with the puppies. While this could be incredibly stressful to other dog moms, we had very easy-going girls who were not in the least bit threatened by others when it came to their puppies. In fact, when Callie's puppies went home at eight weeks, she still had milk and was more than happy to help with nursing Gamine's litter. JJ easily outweighed her siblings by twenty-five percent and seemed happy spending time with Nanny Callie. As a young puppy, JJ loved human interaction and I was drawn to this big, stout girl, even though I wasn't able to say what it was exactly that I liked about her. I put much more thought into most puppies who stayed with us, but it was almost as if I simply knew she was my puppy. After her siblings went to homes, it was evident that JJ maintained a strong bond with Callie. Callie was a sun goddess and fan of fireside naps, and JJ quickly learned to do the same. In JJ's early months, it was clear she had two moms who would play with her and teach her the ways of the world. Watching these beautiful relationships provided a good balance to grief for my own mom.

Learning important life lessons from Nanny Callie: swimming, retrieving, and playing in the never-ending celebration of being a dog.

Back at work, I was aware that one of my home hospice clients, Monika, who had her own black female Labrador, especially loved Callie's visits. This was an exception to the rule of not bringing a therapy dog while visiting homes that had pets. I had been visiting Monika once or twice a week for several months before my mom died and continued to do so afterward. Pets know when their people are doing poorly, and it can wear on them. Callie provided this black Lab with her own kind of therapy during our visits, giving her some lighthearted, pure dog time. Monika, her husband, and their dog lived out in the country and were next to a pasture with ponies and a small Highland cow, the most adorable shaggy thing I have ever seen. I wanted to take her home every time I saw her. One autumn day, my gentle, well-natured therapy dog went on high alert, barking out warning after warning at the cow. Mind you, we had been visiting every week for months, while this cow calmly hung out in the pasture. Apparently, on this day, she seemed menacing to Callie. Dogs are funny that way—you just never know what is going to happen. Monika and I laughed about it, a welcome distraction on a day when we had to have a difficult talk about her disease progression, symptoms, and her increasing weakness.

Shortly before Thanksgiving, during our routine visit, Monika was petting Callie and talking to her when suddenly she asked, "What is this lump on her neck?" What irony it was to have a hospice client with cancer bring this to my attention. How on earth had I missed it? It was huge and my heart sank to my feet. While human medicine and vet medicine can be different, many of the findings are not. We waited for the biopsy to return, but in my gut, I knew it wasn't good. Not my heart dog, I had thought, not the one who was my companion through thick and thin, teaching me how much a dog can make a difference when someone is facing the end of life. The one who helped me make it through Mom's illness and death. Not my girl, please no.

The biopsy results revealed exactly what both the vet and I thought they would. Lymphoma. In people, sometimes treatment can give a few years, but animals have a relatively shorter lifespan than we do. Daily chemotherapy and radiation treatments meant it could buy us maybe four to six months, although there was no guarantee. I was an ICU nurse before changing to hospice, and I witnessed and was a part of the technology that could keep humans alive at all costs. Because of this, I strongly believe that regardless of whether you are treating people or pets, just because we can give extravagant and sometimes invasive treatments, doesn't mean we always should. My hospice philosophy transferred from my patients to our pets. My husband and I chose not to pursue aggressive treatment for this cancer, as it was very advanced. Instead, we made sure Callie had the best possible days left and we were blessed to spend another two and a half months together. She continued to come to work with me and any food restrictions were lifted. The hospice staff made sure she was pampered each day. As one staff member remembered, "If treats could have made her be well, she would be with us still." Each day she got to swim, play, and gopher hunt to her heart's content. Personally, I think swimming in January is nuts, but she loved it. It wasn't just the humans in her life that supported her; during her last month, both Gamine and JJ would cuddle close to Callie, something they didn't often do. They also could sense when she needed some space, but would still stay nearby. It was touching to watch.

Sticking close to my Nanny Callie. I learned from the best, and she taught me a lot in a very short time.

I believe our job as good owners and good stewards of our animals is to know when it is time to let go. I knew Callie would tell me when it was time, but I had to have the strength and fortitude to hear her and act when she was ready. It's never easy, but I knew it was my responsibility not to let her suffer on my account of not wanting her to go. She wasn't feeling very good the last week of her life, but she loved to have her rubdowns, especially from our hospice massage therapists. She lost her appetite, but would eat small amounts of specially made food for a few days. She was spending more time sleeping, but clearly wanted to be with me each day. We made one last visit to Monika out in the country, so she could say her goodbyes. The next day, it was a struggle for Callie to get into the car. After I made some visits while she waited for me, Callie finally just gave me the look. I could tell in her eyes she was tired, her body was worn out, and I had to listen to her. I called the hospice office to see if people wanted me to bring her in for a last goodbye. They did, although I know that was very difficult on so many people, not just me. Somehow, she continued to comfort those who knew they would be mourning her loss very shortly. I called ahead to the vet office before bringing her in and simply said, "It's time." In the vet's client rooms, with her head on my lap, Callie settled in for that long sleep and took her last breath. She was six and a half years old and only with us for five of those years, but oh, what a glorious ride it was.

At the tender young age of four months, JJ became my therapy puppy, hopefully destined for great things. Her nanny and mentor, Callie, left big paw prints to fill on my heart and on the lives of everyone in our community, and only time would tell if JJ would be a good fit. This puppy and her sweet mother helped us all get through some very sad months at home and at work.

Callie's tribute video summed it up nicely. "Companion, good Mommy, sun goddess, mooch, therapy dog, pond scum, nanny, bird dog, kennel hostess, did I say mooch? She played hard and worked hard, seeing special hospice patients until the day before she let us know it was time to say goodbye. Callie has taught us many life lessons along the way. Gone from us now, but forever in our hearts."

My hospice client, Monika, who first found the lump in Callie's neck, came up with the idea of having a fund in Callie's name. Because of the logistics of having two separate hospice funds, there was some resistance to the idea, but Monika was dismissive of the obstacles, reminding me of my stubbornness when it came to starting that therapy dog program at the inpatient hospice center so many years ago. I could only smile at her determination. She donated in Callie's name and then persistently corresponded with those who would make the decision, pressuring them to accept the plan. This went on for some time, even as Monika grew weaker. In the meantime, when I made my nursing visits, I began to bring JJ with me. Monika was thrilled to participate in JJ's early training, and silly puppy hijinks helped to lighten some of the sadness. Shortly before she died, Monika finally got confirmation that Callie's Fund had been officially established. She was proud of what she had done, and I was very grateful for her idea and support.

Callie's Fund specifically addresses pet issues in relation to hospice patients and their families, and supports hospice patients through our hospice's pet therapy program. When it was formally set up, the goals was to help families become proactive about the care of animals when a loved one is facing death. This meant creating service opportunities for community volunteers, subsidizing boarding fees and supplies, and helping to get a pet rehomed. We use Callie's Fund to pay for the ongoing needs of therapy dogs on service as well, and my long-term goal is to get a robust and consistent group of volunteer pet therapy teams visiting at the Hospice House and in various settings in the community. As helpful and supportive as JJ is for everyone, there is no way to be available 24/7. Shortly after Callie's Fund was established, we were awarded a $5,000 grant from the Oregon Animal Health Foundation. Thanks to this generosity, we can provide for various needs such as assistance with veterinarian fees, supplying pet food and sundries for patients and families, and supplying pet care needs for those visiting the Hospice House. Callie's fund also paid for the care of Syd, the Hospice House's outdoor therapy cat.

Over the years, our hospice staff has frequently gone out of their way to assist and donate to our patients and families to provide for their pets, as well as rehoming animals whose owners have died. Callie's Fund has become an extension of that generosity, and we are all grateful to have this resource available. It was not uncommon to sit in IDT discussing a dying patient only to be told about their dog or cat, who will soon need a new home. While family members and friends often come through at the last minute to find a home for a pet, our staff was stepping in if needed. At some point, we knew we would hit the saturation point on rehoming pets, so we began to work with a local no-kill shelter where Callie's Fund will pay for the admission and subsequent adoption fees.

We keep brochures about Callie's Fund, which displayed a photo of Callie prominently, out in the Hospice House foyer. One person who recently visited came up to me in a panic. He had met JJ some months ago and had not noticed the brochure then. While he was waiting to visit one of our patients, he had read the brochure and—unable to easily recognize the difference between JJ and her nanny Callie—he was certain the dog he had met had died. I woke JJ up so she could say hello and as she gave him one of her hugs, he was almost in tears. It was a reminder to me of how much animals can bolster the human soul.

When we built the Hospice House, we knew we would be allowing people to bring their pets to visit. We wanted to include an enclosed, safe place for their people to take them outside. Due to the amazing generosity of the local community, almost all the materials and labor were donated. Since it rains a lot in Oregon, we wanted it to be a covered area so people could stay out of the rain, and we were able to come up with a design that matched the style of the Hospice House. We now have one beautiful area outside that we call Callie's Corner for our therapy dogs and visiting dogs to enjoy. There is a bench under the covered area that was placed in honor of one of our hospice nurses, Charmaine, who died a few months before Callie. Charmaine was a great lover of dogs, and I'm sure she would have loved this space. Under the covered area, I painted four paw prints in each corner with the names of the four staff hospice dogs so far, Marfa, Callie, Gamine, and JJ, as a tribute to the comfort they have and continue to provide for so many. Phoebe, the Cardigan Corgi, will also have her paw print painted in Callie's Corner, as will future hospice therapy dogs.

As hard as Callie's death was on hospice staff at the time, those who spent time with her have very fond memories so many years later:

"She could always tell when I was having a painful day and would sneak into my office and lay her head on my lap."

Another staff member described her as "a lover of people, a gentle soul, big heart, intuitive, an amazing nanny and auntie to all the litters of pups. She was my first introduction to therapy dogs. What a sweet and loveable girl!"

"Her ability as a caregiver to know exactly when you needed that extra love. Thank you for seeing when I needed it, as well as all the love you spread all over."

"I miss giving her massages during IDT. It was my best start of the week spending those few moments with her."

"I have many memories, including how sweet she was with the kitten I had in my office. Also, how she would sometimes come lay down in our little office while I worked at my computer until you came to find her. And her soulful look as she gazed up at me. She made me laugh with some of her fun outfits and she had a magnificent and curly coat. She bounded around with such joy as a youngster. I loved her and the thought of her death still brings tears to my eyes!"

"Tracy, I wanted to thank you personally for bringing Callie into our lives. She brought a lightness into this agency. In the years since I have worked here, I have never seen any being, two legged or four, bring this staff together like Callie did."

What a legacy. My heart dog will forever be with me. Thank you, Callie, for all that you taught me along the way. It was a joy having you in our lives.

8

About nine months after our Hospice House opened for business, a black cat made an appearance on the property. I hadn't been expecting any stray animals in our parking lot, so JJ was off leash as we were walking into work. This was the first cat JJ had ever seen, and this amazing creature fascinated her so she darted over to investigate him. They had a bit of a disagreement—he hissed at her and ran. She, of course, saw this as the best game ever and sped off after him. When it was clear the cat was going to be a repeat visitor, JJ and I had many "training opportunities," so I could teach her not to chase him and to be calm in his presence. It never looks good to have a therapy dog handler screeching her dog's name, while her usually well-behaved animal completely ignores that "recall" business. JJ referred to the cat as Tuna Breath until the humans around determined the cat wasn't leaving and needed a proper name.

Kitty! I can't help it. He comes right over to us and then hisses at me if I move before he takes off. I'm sure he wants to play chase, right?

In the beginning, for a few months, the cat would come and go. We all figured it was a neighborhood cat that would come for a visit and enjoy the food put outside for it. Early on, it was obvious how much this cat enjoyed interacting with people. If the therapy dogs were polite, they were tolerated, but our cat certainly was not a big dog fan. After scanning for a microchip and checking throughout the neighborhood, no one claimed to know anything about the cat and we decided it was time for a visit to the vet. It turned out we had been adopted by a male cat, and after his health exam and vaccinations, it was time to officially give him a name. The hospice staff had a naming contest and ultimately, he was named Sydney, because he reminded many of the cat in the children's book, *Six-Dinner Sid*. In this book, sneaky Sid has six different people who thought he belonged to them, and he gets meals from them all. For a while, our Sydney would come and go like this and we all figured he was getting some good food from other places too. As he settled in and clearly indicated he was going to stay, we spent a lot of time and effort to get JJ to behave nicely around him. It took quite a bit of convincing that he was not her personal play-date partner. Every time we went in and out of the building, JJ got to practice walking off leash next to me as we walked next to Syd. We did sit-stays and down-stays next to him as well as practiced the "leave it" command. Treats were a great incentive for her to behave, and we went through many a bag in those first few months.

Since Syd arrived, we have had several visitors comment that he "needed to be saved" or he "should go live with a family." Early on, when we were concerned about him not having a real home, and before the auspicious vet visit and his naming, one of our couriers took Syd home, intending to take him in as a family member. The next morning, the man woke to find Syd missing. When the courier came to make his morning delivery to the Hospice House, there was Syd, sitting near our front door. Somehow, he had escaped the courier's house and walked almost three miles through the night back to us. That was when we knew Syd was with us by choice. As someone said, "You didn't adopt Syd, he adopted you." Through Callie's Fund, we bought him a mini house, filled it with bedding and a heated pad for wintertime, and our medical director made a wood plaque with his name on it. Syd's house is situated just outside the front door of the Hospice House, away from the wind, yet close enough for easy access to staff and visitors. Callie's Fund also provides all of his food, vet care, and supplies. We tried to give him a cooling pad one unseasonably hot summer, but he turned his nose up and reclined on the hot concrete. During one snowy winter, which is unusual for this area of the country, one of the home health nurses was making a visit and was concerned Syd would get too cold. She wanted to buy a sweater for him. It was well-meant, but we had to explain he had a heated house and a sweater would be a safety concern as he hunted the fields around the property and could get tangled up in a fence. We assured her that he is regularly checked on.

Syd showed up on our door-step and adopted us all. He is a cat with an amazing intuition. Over the years, we have heard several people who think he needs to be "rescued," but like me, he's living the good life.

While Syd and JJ developed a tolerance for one another, Syd began channeling JJ's incredible mooching skills. He talks to most everyone who approaches the building and swears he is starving and has not been fed for days. The first winter his weight shot up, and he certainly wasn't going to freeze with that healthy extra layer of fat. We got to the point where we needed to lock up the cat food, asked visitors not to give him extra food, and designated only two people to feed him. JJ's favorite part of Syd's mealtime is the cookie she gets from the staff for parity. I still don't know how she taught them that trick, but morning cat feeding time is a highlight for her.

While it was clear he did not appreciate affection from the therapy dogs, Syd adores humans. He is fond of wandering the parking lot, meowing at people and even jumping in their cars at times. As one visitor remarked, "When I met the cat outside, I thought he worked for the hospice. He really does go to your car and bring you up to the front door. What a sweet baby." Another commented, "That little kitty has welcomed so many people to the Hospice House. I'm sure he has learned how to comfort those who need it." Over the years, visitors have enjoyed not only interacting with both Sydney and JJ individually but also watching them interact with one another. When JJ is feeling full of herself, it's common to watch her run circles around Syd, while he stands his ground looking thoroughly unimpressed with such shenanigans. She also has been known to race to the front door after being let outside for a break, making a sharp right turn to grab a bite of Syd's food. Recently, the game of sneaking a bite of cat food has morphed into a stealthy sneak attack when letting her out into the field during her break time. She can do her business and then very casually skirt the field under the cover of some very tall grass, only to find herself in the parking lot, a few steps away from that cat food. By the time I was on to her, the bowl was empty with not one ounce of shame on her face. Clearly, I take longer to train, as she used this method at least five or six times before I remembered about it during her first breaks of the day.

In the three years Syd spent helping our families and visitors, we have heard some incredible stories about him. We had a visitor to the Hospice House one morning who was not feeling well. On the drive in, this older gentleman had rolled the car windows down to get some air. Our hospice outpatient phone line received a call from him from the parking lot, and one of our hospice nurses went outside to see him. They called 911, and he was transported to the hospital. We didn't know how he was doing until a few days later when he came to our facility to talk to us.

When we met with him, he told a remarkable story—he insisted that Sydney had saved his life. This gentleman was sitting in the driver's seat of his truck with the windows rolled down having a lot of difficulty. Syd jumped into the truck and onto his lap, then began meowing and pawing at him, stimulating the man enough to muster the energy to make that phone call to us inside. Had Syd not helped him, he was certain he would not have called us. Afterward, I sent out an e-mail to those staff members not present that day. A prompt and comedic response came back to my inbox. "Needed a quick cat scan was all. Syd should get a merit badge at least." Have I mentioned that humor is a great way to get through life?

Syd is not my only experience with cats in hospice. When I started as an inpatient hospice nurse back in the early '90s in Washington State, there was a resident Himalayan cat named Prince that was a wonder to see in action. There have been many stories shared about intuitive animals and their relationships with people, and even a book written about a cat who lived in a nursing facility and would spend time with those who were dying. However, to witness firsthand the power of this human-animal bond was humbling and amazing. As a new hospice nurse, I learned to watch which patients Prince paid the most attention to. We could count on him to point out the next person who was actively dying by perching on the window seat in their room. He never bothered the patient unless invited, instead, he just stood watch. On occasion, he would vigil outside the room, and invariably if I quizzed the family, I would learn that patient did not like cats. If you aren't a cat person, believe me, cats can sense this from miles away. So, Prince was a respectful gent for those non-cat people, but he clearly still felt the need to be close by. The hardest night shifts would be when I had to watch him go back and forth between two rooms, where he couldn't settle and be with just one person. This would frustrate him to no end, and it looked exhausting. One of my colleagues at the time has a favorite Prince story. "The patient was an elderly woman who had a devoted, long-term husband but had never had kids. They had two older cats that they doted on. I don't recall her diagnosis but she was cognitively intact and had declined to the point that her husband could no longer care for her so she agreed to come into our hospice center. After a week or so she had continued to decline, sleeping for longer periods. She was not fully aware of her surroundings, except for her wonderful husband and the cat on the window seat. A day or two before she died, her husband sadly told us that one of their cats at home had died and he had decided he wasn't going to tell her.

"That day Prince began standing watch on the bed, initially at the foot and then slowly moving up to above her pillow. He left the room for short periods and always returned to his station. The next morning, he moved down to the side of her pillow and placed his head on the patient's shoulder and that is where he stayed for several hours until she died. Even at that point, he was not inclined to move off the bed as we bathed and powdered "his lady," making it very clear by yowling when put out in the hall with the door closed. When her body was ready and the door re-opened, he entered to stand at the foot of the bed while the patient was transferred to the gurney. Prince also joined the Walkout by leading the way to the front door, stopping at the outer edge of the driveway where he sat until the funeral vehicle was out of sight. He then disappeared for a few hours, coming back for dinner. I think he found somewhere quiet and private to recharge his battery."

While Syd is an outdoor cat, there are occasions when he sneaks inside. Sometimes he does so because his breakfast is woefully late and he needs to remind the hired help they are slacking. Most of the time it's because Syd wants to be inside near the room where someone is actively dying. Just as I once watched Prince vigil with people, Syd has spent time on beds and even with patients in wheelchairs who ended up dying not very long after his visits. Typically, when he has snuck inside, it has been at night and the staff finds him on the bed of someone getting close to death. As with Prince, sometimes Syd seems to be aware of things we are missing. Recently, we were caring for a woman who would go outside in her wheelchair. When I came in one morning, I was informed she passed the previous night, surprising us since she wasn't showing signs that death was imminent. Apparently, on my one day off, Syd had crawled up into her lap outside and spent quite a bit of time with her. We all just nodded our heads in understanding, while also joking we hoped Syd wasn't going to give any of us his special attention quite yet.

Syd's motto is clearly, "Cats rule, dogs drool." He probably prefers the days none of the dogs show up. I will never give up on our relationship though. One day, he might just cave to my charms.

We had a patient who was with us for just a brief time on a day when JJ and I had off. The family of this patient thought their mom might die during transport, but she made it to the Hospice House and was made comfortable and had all her people around her at the end. This patient had a huge family and many of them had visited her that afternoon and evening. Several stayed, including one who went to sit in his car. In the early hours of the morning, this man was awakened by Syd, who was persistently and loudly meowing outside his vehicle. He decided to go back inside to his mother's room, arriving just shortly before she passed. All her children were present, holding hands and standing around their mother's bed as she took her last breath. They credit Syd for helping make those final family moments possible.

One staff member shared with me the story of a family of an actively dying patient and how through the shift Sydney would approach and offer comfort to their loved ones when they would go outside for a break. Stories of Syd's interactions with patients and loved ones warms everyone's hearts, even for those who are not fans of cats, and Syd spends time with staff as well. One of our night nurses has an end-of-shift ritual that includes not just spending time snuggling first with JJ but also stopping to visit Syd outside before leaving. One of our Hospice House volunteers described his tradition with the cat: "Syd and I have a ritual. As I arrive for my shift each week, I call him out of his house and give him some love. This is repeated as I leave after my shift is finished." So many staff members have stories like this and are always pleased to be greeted in the morning as Syd strolls the parking lot checking in with all the humans.

We had a young woman recently at the Hospice House for several weeks. She was very ill with cancer that she had been fighting for several years. She started as a home hospice patient and came into the Hospice House for symptom control. She ended up declining and staying here approximately one month until her death. This lady had two school-age children at home. At the time of her death, the family decided to have the eleven-year-old son come in for his final goodbye. Tina, this young man's grandmother and the patient's mom, eloquently told the story: "He was only 11 years old, but he knew what he needed. He wanted—no, needed—to see his mom one more time after she had taken her last breath. Impossible to think about. How does a young boy be brave enough to walk in to say goodbye to his mom, one last time?

"Saying 'goodbye' had begun weeks earlier, but this final moment held the weight that would only reveal itself in the days and weeks to come. But, in that moment, a brave young boy walked in and faced his mom for the last time on this side of heaven. The bond between a child and his mother made the impossible possible. He was choosing this moment and knew he needed it.

"After some private time, he held his head high and walked with us all as we accompanied her out of the building. Surrounded by the staff that had so skillfully and lovingly been caring for her, we all stood and watched as she was driven away into the darkening skies. We comforted him. We comforted each other and as we began to thank the staff for their love and care, we noticed our grandson walking away by himself. He found his way to the edge of the parking lot and sat down on the curb under the streetlight.

"Not surprised that he would want a moment alone, we just stood by and respectfully watched. Sydney, the resident outdoor cat, must have been at his post that night watching. Almost as though he was being called, he took off on a run over to our grandson. He slowed only as he reached him and began to nuzzle up against him. Did Syd know that our boy loved cats? He scooped him up into his arms and held Syd while he sobbed quietly. Sydney stayed in his lap until he was ready to rejoin us. This unexpected comforter left us all with our jaws open. The staff was equally surprised to see Syd offering comfort. 'Syd must be taking lessons from JJ.'" Even in sorrow, laughter can be found in the innocence of a child and a comforting cat. Thank you, Sydney!

Silly cat. I do my best to show him how to enjoy life and let his fur down, but no! He's gotta go get himself all in a hissy fit. I was doing donuts around him today during break time. At least our antics made some grieving families laugh for a few minutes. I am here to serve.

"One vivid memory for me is of your amazing kitty Sydney. I remember your stories about how he had also positively impacted other visitors with his presence at the Hospice House. For me, Syd became my Quan Yin of compassion because he seemed to be 'walking with me' the last ten days that I was there. The only way for me to explain his 'energy' is to tell you that for the last two years while acting as the main caregiver for my aunt, I did not allow myself to cry or become emotional because it was so important that I remain stoic and focused on her comfort. My aunt had been diagnosed with bladder cancer in January 2013 and I had been by her side through numerous difficult surgeries and painful, invasive office procedures. So, I held back my tears. That is, until our second day at the Hospice House when I stopped and bent down to pet Syd. For some unknown reason, Syd suddenly decided to gently climb up onto my back while I knelt beside him and gently stroked his fur. He peacefully laid down between my shoulder blades, softly purring, his green eyes closed in calm repose, his velvety black tummy and pulsating heartbeat warming my back on that frigid day. Suddenly, my tears began to flow, at long last. I will be forever grateful for the warmth and true expression of compassion that Syd was able to convey in his own way. I know in my heart that Syd sensed my deep emotional pain. His abiding presence during those ten days was precious, reassuring and immensely uplifting for me. I hope this sharing brings you joy because joy and gratitude are what I felt when leaving the Hospice House for the last time on that dark, icy morning. Syd was

nestled in the back of his house as I walked out through the front doors after my aunt died. I thanked him for his amazing caring and the special kinship we shared. I truly believe he is a part of hospice for a reason."

I must give Super Kitty his props. He's a cool cat, even if he doesn't appreciate the affection from the therapy dogs around here. Treats for the Hospice Kitty Syd. You've done good work!

9

I often say our household is like a zoo, and as the zookeepers, we often can only shake our heads at the animals we share our lives with. JJ is only one of the large cast of characters I have had the pleasure of spending my life with.

This wild ride all started with a puppy named Dash. I had become interested in field retriever games, but the Golden I owned didn't have the gumption for training to perform at the more advanced levels. I wanted my next puppy to come from the right lines for playing these games, as it was so interesting to watch these dogs do what they were bred for. After researching different breeders and meeting people who got their dogs from a breeder in Minnesota, I drove out to pick up this wild little puppy. Golden Retrievers range in color from a very light gold to a dark gold-red. It was obvious this guy was on the dark end of the spectrum, and his registered name became Wildfire Dash O' Tabasco. His name suited him—life with him was wild, fiery, and spicy at times.

Dash was an independent, curious, and adventurous puppy from the moment I brought him home. His attitude was "join me if you'd like, but I'm headed out to explore the world." When he was home on breaks from retriever school, he would keep me company and make me laugh. He turned out to be more dog than I could ever handle by myself in competition, and he made sure we had a grand adventure together.

It was because of this goofy dog that I met my husband. Tellus was a professional retriever trainer whom I met while running Dash at a hunt test. I had grown up with all sorts of animals, and once I heard his stories, I discovered Tellus had as well, and was as much of an animal freak as I was. He grew up in Sacramento, California and when he was young, he and his brother essentially had their own wildlife collection on the roof of their house. Anything they could catch lived up there. They cared for birds, squirrels, snakes and even an owl, collecting whatever each species needed to live and thrive. Tellus can still rattle off details including what each animal ate, what it needed for its habitat, and how long of a life span it had. His parents knew nothing about the rooftop safari "until the lady next door ratted us out." In his early teens, Tellus would walk the alley in the neighborhood, letting dogs out of their yards to take them for a walk, returning them before their people would get home from work. That probably wouldn't go over so well these days, but back then the dogs were happy, he was happy, and the owners were none the wiser, although they may have wondered why their dogs seemed so tired. Tellus also was known for playing with a guard dog at one of the local vet hospitals. Apparently, he and the dog did not get the memo that the dog was supposed to be protection trained and not let a thirteen-year-old kid climb in to play with him. When he was in high school, he had wanted a horse but was told no. The enterprising guy that he was, bought a horse for "fifty dollars down, fifty dollars a month" and boarded it down the road. Again, his parents were none the wiser until his dad found a saddle and the rest of the horse tack in his trunk one day. He was busted.

My favorite stories are from his time working at the Science Center in Sacramento. Tellus was the only one on staff who could brush Wiley, the coyote. He would take Wiley home and walk him on a leash in one of the local parks. He would pass tough guys out walking their Dobermans who would freak out at what was on the end of his leash. The Science Center was next to a driving range, and it wasn't unusual for Wiley to get loose and run to the driving range to chase golf balls. Tellus would then have to go catch him. He would also bring Tippy the fox home and walk her on a leash as well. Tellus and Tippy would play hide and seek in the Science Center and she would run donuts around him, just as our dogs do today. I'm told he had to be very careful with Benny the badger, as he could go from nice to grumpy in six seconds flat. He would talk to the animals in their own language, and they would talk back to him. Years after he stopped working there, he walked into the Science Center one day and all the animals started scurrying about, doing donuts, chattering, and throwing a collective fit. No one could figure out what was going on until the director looked over and said, "Oh it's just Tellus."

I think it was inevitable that the Crazy Dog Lady and the Creature Freak would partner up. Tellus has a long history of pranking not only animals but kids as well. Both are drawn to him, and his antics always have them coming back for more. When we were all in Montana for Mom's memorial, he loved to give our nephews grief calling Trevor by the name Bob. This three-year-old towhead would stamp his feet and say, "I'm not Bob!" To which he would be told, "OK, Bob." On and on it would go. One day, his older brother was eating dipping candy that turned his lips and tongue purple, which of course, earned him the name "Purple Lips." We knew we would be keeping a puppy from "Mom's Litter," so we decided her registered name would be "Calhoun's I'm Not Bob," and her call name was Trev. We also kept a male puppy and named him Bob. For family harmony, we knew we needed to name our puppy out of Gamine's litter after our other nephew. How in the heck do you come up with a girl name from Jaret? We settled on JJ, and her registered name is "Calhoun's The Color Purple"—this is how JJ got her name. Years later, the boys are still Bob and Purple Lips to us, much to their chagrin.

Tellus frequently travels the country while running or judging retriever events. For several years, he transported the dogs in a horse trailer equipped with eighteen crates and an air conditioner. It was always funny to watch people walk by the trailer and if they got too close, our black Lab Max would let out a series of warning barks. It would scare the heck out of people who weren't expecting dogs in a horse trailer. Tellus is known around the country in the retriever world as a dog trainer and is well known among that demographic. He is frequently stopped when visiting the south and will have people who recognize him follow and want to meet him. He often travels alone, so I would only hear about these things. When I was traveling back with him from one event in the south, a car zipped past us on the interstate and then suddenly put on their brakes. I warned Tellus there might be a highway patrolman up ahead, but he shook his head and laughed as we watched the car ease back toward us. As I looked over, the car full of people started smiling and waving madly at him. Luckily, he has me to make sure he doesn't get a big head over such attention.

Long before JJ was ever a twinkle in her mama or daddy's eye, Tellus and I had some great adventures. We always had at least sixteen to twenty dogs with us as we traveled from event to event. People frequently ask us how we have such attentive dogs. Well, Labs and Goldens love their food, and keeping a big box of dog biscuits at hand means our dog truck is the doggie equivalent of an ice cream truck rolling into the neighborhood. Our dogs are also used to having a lot of playtime. Playtime is extremely important in building and maintaining working relationships with dogs. Because of this, they will follow Tellus anywhere, whether he is on a quad, tractor, or lawn mower. This has gone on for all the years we have been together.

Meanwhile, each winter I secretly do a snow dance in hopes of at least one snowstorm. Secretly, because the dear husband of mine is not the least bit happy to deal with the white stuff when it shows up. It is rare in the Pacific Northwest to have any snow, so when it does happen the dogs have a blast. There is nothing more fun than throwing snowballs for retrievers as they pile into a snow bank to try to retrieve them. To this day, we continue to share our lives with a variety of Labs and Goldens. They are at all ages—many have retired from competition and are just enjoying life, while some are up and coming young dogs.

Tellus likes to tease me about how I pamper the dogs, though he'll do it himself. On a trip back from my parents' house, three of the Labs were going to sleep in the back of our small truck one night, and Tellus wanted to make it soft for them, and so he spread out a sleeping bag filled with goose down. Come morning, when I lifted the back of the truck topper, there was a tornado of feathers with three down-coated black Labs in the middle of it all, their expressions all said, "No idea what happened." In retrospect, it might not have been the best idea to put hunting dogs in with an item made of goose feathers. It was such a mess, but I imagine they had the best time, like little kids jumping up and down on a bed, laughing and giggling. There are so many times I wish we could have these episodes on tape.

Tellus is a bit horrified to know JJ's nickname for him on social media is, "The Man Who Makes Me Wiggle" or "Wiggle Man," which has been shortened to "WM" for the sake of decorum. Every dog gets wiggly and excited when Tellus is around, whether he has been gone for days or minutes. It was evident long before JJ was around how much all dogs absolutely love him, though he is a disciplined trainer. When he was running one of the Super Retriever Series events in Reno, Nevada, which is a televised event, the producer thought it would be nice for the final series handlers to kneel beside one or two of their dogs and do an introduction. Tellus knew if he did this, the dogs would think it was time for fun and games, but the producer insisted. Sure enough, even though he was telling them "no," once he knelt down, Max and Blue expected it was playtime. This SRS episode showed all the trainers introducing their dogs who were calmly seated next to them, but they kept flashing back and forth to Max and Blue, jumping around, blowing off the "sit" command and trying to get in Tellus' lap to lick his face. You finally could hear him say "Can I stand up now?" Serious dog trainer. It still gives me the giggles.

Dash quickly became Tellus' dog, bonding with him intensely, as all of the dogs do, but his independent, stubborn canine self earned him a rash of unprintable nicknames and put my husband's training skills to a serious test. In competition, Dash was known to go on autopilot and flip his handler the paw. Apparently, he could look at the situation and come up with a far better plan on how to do his retrieving than Tellus ever could. I'm so glad I was not the one on the line while he embarrassed me. Tellus is far better at laughing at dogs at times like this than I am. Dogs can really keep you humble when you compete, but Dash was an overachiever at doing things his own way.

Dash and Max, a black Lab male who was far better at following his trainer's rules than Dash ever was, were Tellus' constant companions, often arguing over who got to ride shotgun. Labs typically are more serious about the work they do, while Goldens are frequently known as the class clowns. This held true for Max and Dash when Tellus would use them as his demonstration dogs at events. In Minnesota, at one popular venue called Game Fair, Tellus and two other trainers were demonstrating retriever skills and then letting the kids run the dogs on retrieves. While Tellus was working with Max, he put Dash on a down-stay on an elevated platform. The crowd started giggling and Tellus looked over his shoulder. Dash had crept off the table and was crawling toward him, maintaining his down position the entire time and looking at Tellus as if to say "What? I'm still down." It was like the Three Stooges, every time Tellus would turn back to Max, Dash would belly crawl toward him again while the crowd laughed.

In retriever games at more advanced levels, one of the things the dogs must do is honor the working dog. This means one dog must wait politely while the other one does the retrieving. If the honor dog decides he wants to help his buddy out with the retrieves, he might get points for enthusiasm, but he fails the test. Dash's version of honoring was to eat some grass, roll around (once down a hill), and basically be a goofball while waiting to be excused. Because of an old injury, Dash had to be retired early and just got to do fun, shorter retrieves. When we had a lot of dogs in for training, we participated in the Youth Outdoor Day. Each year 750 kids got to come experience a variety of outdoor activities, including running our dogs on retrieves. Dash was always a favorite because of his silliness, and we had several kids come back year after year and ask for "my dog Dash."

In his later years, Dash became quite vocal when he wanted something. He continued to go with Tellus anywhere he went, riding shotgun, then in the evening when it was time to go in the house, he would dance around and start barking if he thought Tellus was taking too long. He expected to have his commands followed and would bark louder if he was ignored. He wasn't much company when they were on the road together, as Dash would be curled up and snoring before they even left the driveway. At eleven and twelve years old, when Tellus would set up for training, Dash continued to tag along as the exercise was good for him. When retrievers are being trained, one of the things they learn to do is a blind retrieve. The dogs are directed to an area with whistles and hand signals to pick up something they have not seen thrown. Tellus had several dogs he would do this with, so there was a large pile of bumpers at each area, between 250 to 300 yards away, where he and Dash had walked out. You never want to send a dog to an area and not have something for them to pick up, so the number of bumpers at each pile was carefully calculated. As they walked back toward the dog truck, Tellus wasn't paying much attention until he realized Dash wasn't with him. He whistled him in and then realized he had one of the bumpers in his mouth. Dash was proud of himself but wasn't going to give up what pile he stole the bumper from. It meant Tellus had to walk back to the two different locations to figure out where it needed to be replaced. My husband might have been a runner for Nike in his early days, but he's not a fan of long walks today. This is just one of the many examples that led to Dash having so many colorful names.

In the house, Dash would let us know when his water or food bowl was empty, a trait JJ shares today. He would trot out with it in his mouth and plop it at our feet as if to say "Waitress. Service, please." He was a perfect paper shredder, although he never seemed to choose the junk mail, only important documents. He was also persistent at getting what he wanted. I once found him climbing up some steep attic stairs to raid the collection of new training bumpers we had stored away there. He believed in the philosophy "no stick too big" and would often try to drag small trees home, another trait he has passed on through the generations. He was a pro at deconstructing and scattering the firewood pile so that when we wanted to build a fire, we had to go on a scavenger hunt. We would hear noises in the living room and look up to see him dragging a huge dog bed down the hall towards us from the bedroom. JJ always loved when he did this and would jump onto the bed as he dragged her along, grunting and muttering something about "kids." JJ loved her dad, Dash, and would spend as much time as she could with him, especially when it came to swimming time. Her exuberant leaps into the water often meant another dog got dunked.

Woo Hoo! Sneak attack on Daddy-O Dash! Have I mentioned how much I LOVE the water? Well, not bath water, but pond water. COWABUNGA!

Tellus often had to fly to events, which meant leaving Dash home. The dog acted as though this was the worst punishment ever and would wait patiently for the "real deal" to return home. I always felt more comfortable with Dash in the house when I was alone because he was quick to sound an alarm if he was concerned about anything. Over the years, however, I was certain he was just messing with me to get me to come check out whatever he was barking at. One day I heard maniacal barking at the front door and I came running, certain King Kong was about to break into the place. This was one of the times Tellus had flown out and left the dog truck behind. I had moved the truck the night before and because of this, Dash thought his master had returned home. No amount of shushing him would quiet his barking. I took him outside and he ran around, looking in every possible hiding place he could think of while barking "come out, come out where ever you are!" Tellus was known to play hide and seek with him often. Dash and the rest of the dogs thought this was one of the best games ever. But, his master wasn't there, so Dash moped until Tellus returned home, making me feel like I was chopped liver in his eyes. Unless, of course, I had chopped liver, and then I was the bomb. Fickle dog.

Since Callie was my therapy dog and companion, we wanted to get another Golden to do field competition with. We found out about a four-year-old female someone was selling from Quebec in Canada. English is not the primary language in that part of Quebec, French Canadian is, so the communication back and forth was a bit interesting. We only had a photo of Gamine with her nose sticking through a railing and the assurance she had solid training and would be a good candidate for the Master Hunter level of AKC hunt tests. She was the same dark gold-red as Dash and had her hip and elbow clearances. They put her on a plane to Seattle where she had to go through Customs, so I sent Tellus to pick her up. He called to let me know he had her and said, "Um, what kind of dog did you get? She's the funniest looking thing I have ever seen." Oh, my. It turns out she was a hunting dog and not allowed in the house, so she had been exposed to the elements for too long at some point and was missing some of her tail and most of one ear from frostbite. She didn't seem to understand English so she couldn't take orders, and her training level was vastly overstated. Still, she was a happy girl, a joy to be around, and she quickly learned what being a house-dog was all about. While Gamine never did run any hunt tests, she did get to participate in training and she had a ball. She turned out to be a sweet and tolerant mother who also loved all puppies and took to the nanny role just as Callie had. Her sweet demeanor tempered Dash's enthusiasm, independence, and kookiness. We had no idea at the time what a great combination the two of them were, though as JJ got older, she gave us a hint. Many of JJ's siblings have gone on to do therapy or service work, and her young brother Dingle is a certified Search and Rescue canine.

After Callie died, I decided to pursue therapy work not just with JJ, but with Gamine as well. Gamine has always fallen in love with anyone she meets. She can be a bit clingy, so she was perfect for the people who want non-stop petting and unrelenting attention. JJ enjoyed interacting with people, but wasn't quite as "in your face." Having these two personalities allowed me to customize which dog to take to which visit. Gamine was also a hit in the hospice office and people still love to have her come visit today. She's not a good match for staying at the Hospice House like JJ is, simply because no one would ever get any work done due to her insistence on being petted constantly.

When she became a therapy dog and had been spayed, Gamine gained a lot of weight with her more sedentary lifestyle. It didn't help that she was no stranger to the fine art of mooching—JJ comes by this skill honestly. Once the Hospice House opened, my work schedule became too busy to volunteer with two dogs, so I let Gamine retire. As we worked on getting her weight down, she went for long walks and swims. Along the way, no matter where she went, she continued to spread her charm to anyone she met.

Mama Gamine was doing her thing at Starbucks and loving it! She might be retired from therapy work, but she still has the moves, kisses, and love. We talked to a lady in Pasco, Washington for about ten minutes. It turns out that our hospice program took care of her mom a few years ago in Lebanon. What a small world.

As Gamine lost her weight and became spry again, she continued to love interacting with people. I decided to work on getting her re-certified as a therapy dog. By this point, she was twelve years old and mostly deaf. She knew her hand signals for obedience commands such as sit, down, and stay. The challenge was finding a way to get through the recall exercise when she was being petted by another person. Gamine hadn't changed much over the years and still thought hanging out with anyone who would pet her was a great deal never to be passed up. A treat in my pocket would have been such a nice incentive but isn't allowed during the testing. We did make it through our evaluation, although it required a bit of jumping up and down on my part to make sure she came back to me. Due to her age, I planned on doing short visits with her so she didn't get overly stressed or fatigued. I had been making therapy dog visits to a memory care facility with JJ and believed she needed a break. With Gamine's temperament and white, sugar face, I thought she would be a better fit for memory care, and it was true, the residents immediately responded to her.

When I would take JJ to the memory care facility, we would visit with a gentleman who always would reminisce about his dog Amber Lee, who looked very similar to JJ when she was young. On my first visit with Gamine, his eyes absolutely lit up when he saw her and he cried out, "Amber Lee, you've come to see me," and drew Gamine in close to snuggle with him. There were many caregivers nearby when this happened and there was not a dry eye in the house. He told everyone how I was taking care of Amber Lee for him and would bring her to visit. I was deeply touched by his affection for her.

A colleague who works with memory care clients heard this story and said, "You painted the perfect picture! On my memory care unit, I have always said the two things that will brighten the moments of a dementia patient are a baby or a dog. Of course, usually on my unit, a sweet dog is much more settled and tolerant of our patients. Perhaps it is a memory of long ago, or perhaps it is the calmness between the person and the dog for that one moment. No matter how far their dementia has progressed, the smiles, love pats, and hugs shared with a loving therapy dog can help for a few minutes to open up the person's soul. This mutual bond, even if only for a short time, is one of the most touching and amazing things I have ever witnessed. I love this story and have great admiration for sweet Mama Gamine."

Gamine is a character in her own right and she adores Tellus. Of course, what dog doesn't, and her cute face gets her a treat from him every time. She's quite pleased with herself for training him so well. When she is outside, she will scan the property to find him. He's like the ice cream man for her. One summer she decided a laundry basket would make a good dog bed and spent several days napping in it, the way a cat sleeps in a box. She has never met a day she didn't like and she reminds us to live in each moment joyfully. Nine years later, we still laugh when she turns and looks at us with the remainder of her left ear at attention. Tellus always says to her, "Do you hear what I hear?" as she smiles right back at him, not hearing a thing he is saying. I keep telling my husband that it's not good manners for a therapy dog to have her mooching reinforced, but he just laughs. They all know to watch his hands. If he picks his food up with a fork, they stay relaxed. If he picks up food with his hand, they are all on high alert, ready for something to be tossed their way.

One of JJ's older sisters, Ottie, went to live with a family not far from us. Originally, they were going to do field events with her, but she was raised by a teenager who let her live quite the unstructured life. When she was eighteen months old, we received a call asking if she could come back to us. The boy who raised her was going to college and his parents didn't have time for her. As any responsible breeder would, the answer was yes. When she came home, we saw right away that she was like her daddy Dash without the Y chromosome. She had his same spinning moves, used his same sassy bark, and she fit in perfectly with the rest of the zoo. While JJ never destroys any of her toys at work, Ottie can kill a dog toy in no time flat—even the ones designated "for tough chewers." It also became evident in the house that Ottie was lacking some manners and had been allowed to do whatever she wanted. At the time, we had one designated dog couch, and the rest of the furniture was off limits; still, she would fling herself on whatever she wanted and when told no, would give a disdainful glance that clearly said to us "nuh-uh."

Ottie came back to us with a bad habit of trying to catch flies and other bugs, including those with nasty stingers on them. Recently, she ended up with a bad bite on her face, with her muzzle swelling up at least twice the normal size. She was given antihistamines, but by the next morning, she looked horrible. True to my nurse self, when I saw the droopy lip, eye, and ear on her left side, I thought she had a brain tumor or stroke. Nurses go to the worst-case scenario every time—that is if we don't just say, "Nah, you're good. You're not going to die." She had developed something called

Horner's syndrome, which affects facial muscles, often after a trauma. She has residual nerve damage and has a squinty pirate eye and an ear that doesn't come all the way forward, but otherwise is perfectly fine. To this day, she needs an occasional reminder of house rules and her exploring is going to be the end of me. But boy, she is fun just like her dad and is the best mother dog we have ever had.

When I first met Tellus, he had a Jack Russell Terrier named Pinch. In the retriever world, she was known as a "truck dog," a small dog who gets to ride around in the truck and just have fun. Most terriers were originally bred to "go to ground" after burrowing vermin, larger rodents, and even foxes. Jack Russells are described as a dog "full of life and confidence, with a strong voice and fearless nature." Yes, that was Pinch. While in Montana one summer, her prey-drive kicked in so fiercely while hunting a field for voles that she refused to come back to the truck after many, many hours. Tellus finally had to go scoop her up and tell her stop. She had a crazed look in her eyes and it took a while for her to settle. After Pinch died, we only had big dogs for quite some time, until I got a memorable phone call from Tellus, who was at the vet. "So, Dillon got his rabies shot. He didn't need anything else. Oh, and we have a new puppy." Click.

Who goes to the vet with a dog and comes home with a puppy? Our vet is also a Lakeland Terrier breeder and voila! Tellus had a truck dog once again. We named her Goldie after our Super Retriever Series champion yellow Lab who died of cancer in 2007. The newest Goldie was a force to be reckoned with; she quickly crowned herself Queen of the Kennel and boss of all dogs, no matter how big they might be. The American Kennel Club description of this breed is rather amusing: "They are easy to train when their natural instincts are properly channeled, but be careful not to let the dog do the training. Lakelands never tire of strategizing, and they love a good brainteaser. They are an intelligent dog, very capable of formulating a solution to any problem, whether it be to train his people to work around his schedule or stalk the neighborhood squirrels." I'm not sure how amused Dash was at having to share his truck dog status, but he learned to put up with her.

Our zoo has expanded to include other unexpected residents. One winter we had a cat show up on our doorstep, and she was very persistent on getting into the house. All the dogs including JJ were fascinated, as we had never had a cat around before, and JJ hadn't met Syd yet. The canines gave her a wide berth while I tried to figure out where she came from. After scanning her for a microchip, I discovered she belonged to a couple about a mile up the road. She was one of their several barn cats. I returned her, only to have her "knock, knock, knock" at our door one day later. We did this dance about three times before I spoke with the neighbors about letting Abby hang out with us, and over the months, she and the dogs got used to each other. Frequently, she would go out on a walkabout, but would usually return late at night wanting in the house. One evening she simply never came back. We checked with the neighbors, but they hadn't seen her either. We talked about getting another cat and decided starting with a kitten might be better with the crazy pack of dogs we had. We didn't want to rescue a cat that had not been around dogs before, so we waited until the vet techs we knew who fostered were overrun during kitten season.

One morning the hospice dogs—Marfa, Phoebe, and JJ—had a photo shoot for the Hospice Christmas card. It was a day off for us, so I brought along Shylah, my latest puppy. When we arrived at the Hospice House, one of the clerical staff had a scarf around her neck that moved. JJ made a bee-line for what turned out to be a tiny yellow-orange, five-week-old kitten. He was found on the street by her neighbor who was not able to keep him, so she brought him in hoping someone at work would take him home. Tellus happened to be out of town at a retriever event. I gave him a call and decided to take the kitten home after a quick visit to the vet. The moment I brought him into the house, he took charge. At twenty ounces, he strutted down the hall like a boss. We named him Taz, as in the Tasmanian Devil, and put him in a separate room so the dogs wouldn't overwhelm him.

"Where's Taz?" Wiggle Man hasn't met the newest member of the zoo yet since he's away on business and he was concerned about his safety with the big dogs when we are at work. I think it's all good.

After the second day, Taz abandoned his cat room, which was gated off for his protection, and moved in with all the Goldens. When Tellus was concerned about how the tiny kitten was doing, I sent him a video of him snuggling with Dash while being cleaned like a puppy. All the dogs got their turn with him and to this day, he needs to have a dog to cuddle up with at nighttime. He essentially was raised as a Golden Retriever and was affectionately dubbed cat-dog early on. He tended to spend more time snuggling with Dash and JJ, though he could also be found with Mama Gamine and Ottie. Every dog in the house was smitten with this curious little creature and they were very tolerant of his antics. However, within two days, I was seriously questioning the wisdom of raising a 5-week-old kitten and 9-week-old puppy at the same time. Just as I was getting Shylah used to house life as a single puppy and teaching her how to be well mannered, along comes a bouncy, sassy kitten that tempted her every minute of the day. How two small youngsters could make it sound like a thundering herd of elephants running down the hallway was beyond me. Their favorite game was playing fort under the bed until Shylah got too big. They would roll around together playing and when Taz would emerge, his head was soaked from Shylah mouthing him. It was a little wild, but finally, things settled down. The addition of this cat to our group of housedogs has made life much more entertaining.

Tellus and I have amazingly well-tempered dogs, the kind that can all eat from the same bowl without arguing. This was a good thing, as tiny Taz always wanted to stick his head into the food bowls while everyone ate. JJ would even let him come over and lick the bone she was chewing on without an ounce of protest. It probably would be unwise to allow this with most animals, because we have very tolerant dogs. Taz prefers dog toys to cat toys and would frequently make a stash of them under the bed in his secret lair. His favorite game is chase, which usually involves running up to a dog and bopping them on the hip and running away to hide under the bed. He even does this with puppies, but then seems to get extremely annoyed when they follow him to his hiding spot. Taz is skilled at setting up ambushes for JJ and she falls for them every time. He'll hide in some corner and start giving a distressed yowl that ensures she will come running, then he goes for her tail and chases her through the house. This is especially fun when we have a young puppy in the house. Any semblance of control is a hallucination on my part. Taz makes sure that the humans aren't left out of the fun and games; he'll wait under the bed or the couch to swipe at our feet when we walk by. Tellus has several colorful nicknames for cat-dog too.

While Taz does channel his inner cat on occasion, no one has had the heart to let him know he is not a Golden Retriever. He is most bonded to JJ but will sleep with any of the Goldens. He also plays chase, and everyone but Mama Gamine will join in. She just looks at him as if he's lost his mind. We keep Taz indoors, as indoor cats have a longer life span, but since he was always running to the door when I took the dogs outside we trained him to a harness as a kitten. He likes being outside, but obviously thinks it is highly undignified and beneath him to be tied down in such a fashion despite JJ giving him a look as if to say, "Dude, you're one of us, deal with the leash training like a big dog. Channel your inner Golden and put on a happy face."

When Tellus is overrun by the dogs wanting his attention, it is common to hear the announcement: "I'm not a dog person. Go away." In answer, JJ just wiggles and talks even louder to him. I have concluded that while Taz is her therapy cat, my husband is definitely her therapy person. Just a few minutes with him recharges her batteries. It is not uncommon for him to come by the Hospice House midday for a quick visit. She can be sound asleep, but the question "Who's here" has her running for the door. She is so excitable around him he cannot fathom how she is described as quiet and calm at work. At the same time, those at work cannot believe her reaction if he walks in the door. She jumps, does her growly-whiny talk to him, and cannot stop wiggling for the life of her. Our volunteers at the front desk will stare slack jawed in amazement. When she is at home, he can walk out to the kennel and return not five minutes later and she greets him in the same enthusiastic way she would if it had been days since she saw him last. Sometimes he'll tease me, "You know, YOU should greet me this way every time I come in the door." Apparently, I am wiggle challenged.

One of the most difficult things about sharing your life with a pet is that they have a shorter lifespan than we do. Since we have always had so many dogs around us, we have had to say goodbyes more frequently. Sometimes, our dogs like Callie have had much too short of a time with us, while others like Max and Dash enjoyed a long lifetime. I always pay attention to our senior dogs with a watchful hospice eye. We do our best to keep their quality of life as good as possible while acknowledging that eventually, something is going to give. It is not uncommon for our pets to hide an end stage disease until symptoms are full blown and their time left is short and there are few treatment options. It would be so much easier if we could ask them, "How are you feeling?" and they could actually answer.

Dash was just approaching thirteen years old when we noticed him slowing down a bit. When he was six, he was hit by a car and fractured his femur. Since then, the hardware in his leg caused arthritis over the years. He was gimpy if he overdid any exercise and was slow to get up in the morning, doing his old man shuffle until his muscles warmed up. In people years, he was eighty-two and had earned those stiff bones. As a young dog, he ran so hard when retrieving, if he tripped and fell, it was scary. At one field trial in the derby, I wasn't sure if he was going to get back up after somersaulting and landing hard on his back. He also fancied himself Superman, leaping wide ditches in a single bound. Unfortunately, this usually ended up with him careening chest first into the other side of said ditch. If we had x-rayed his skeleton as an old guy, it probably would have shown arthritis in all his joints from those spectacular spills in his younger days. After he turned thirteen, we counted each day as a bonus. He still was sassy and got to spend time with his puppies, rolling around and wrestling with them. He had been Tellus' duck hunting dog and still perked up at any possibility that he might go back into the field to do some retrieving with him.

At times like these, I am thankful to be such a longtime hospice nurse, extremely attuned to the subtle symptoms of decline and the need to keep a watchful eye to maintain comfort. By this point, Dash fatigued extremely quickly, as our hospice patients do during their last days. He was no longer interested in basic dog food but did enjoy hot dogs, bacon, and ice cream. Loss of appetite is normal in a dying body, whether human or animal. My focus was making sure he was comfortable for his remaining days and to gently prepare my husband for what was to come. Several people had asked me what was wrong with him and I still don't know. We chose not to put him through a battery of diagnostic tests, as his symptoms were telling all of us enough and in his last few days, there really would have been nothing to do with the information. It could have been a malignancy with some muscle wasting, weight loss, and weakness or it could have been other organ failure that accompanies an aging body. I see this routinely during my work as many older people come into our Hospice House after a very rapid decline with a probable diagnosis of cancer or organ failure. Most people choose to quit poking and prodding so they can have some restful days at the end. Data can be helpful, but when someone is dying, we often ask "To what end?"

As we had with Max one year earlier, we made sure that Dash could have that one final retrieve while he still was willing and able. I knew time was short and, without saying why I was very insistent we get this done, we made a special trip with all the dogs for this. It was very much a circle of life occasion—where we had different generations with us. Dash had his last retrieve and enjoyed it, although one retrieve was all he had the energy for. After this, while he rested in the air conditioning with his puppy mama Gamine, his daughters, son, and granddaughter played with the rest of the dogs doing fun water retrieves. It was very reminiscent of our hospice patients' families who gather to say their goodbyes, while the kids or grand-kids play in our family room.

The next night, while Tellus was out of town, Dash started having trouble breathing. It is common for hospice patients to have breathing difficulties in the last hours or days, requiring medications to keep them comfortable during the dying process. We have different options for our animals. As a hospice nurse, I know exactly when someone is suffering and when he or she needs medications to help their symptoms. If Dash were my hospice patient, I would be pulling out the very strong stuff to try to help with symptom management. I knew exactly what needed to happen and I wasn't going to make him wait any longer. It probably was better that Tellus was out of town as it would have been so very hard on him. My family had started with just Dash and I, and ended the same way, with his head in my lap as Dash, our knucklehead, gently took his last breath.

As all pet owners know, our lives are usually shorter than our people's. We pack a lot of love, affection, fun, joy, and naughtiness into the time we have. Along the way, we teach our people about loyalty, love, the importance of play, how to live in the moment, the importance of a good nap, and the art of the enthusiastic tail wag. "Good dogs are with us for a little while to teach us how to love like it is our job, because it is." We trust in you and we will let you know when it is time to say goodbye. It is my wish for all animals to be able to say their goodbyes surrounded by dignity, respect, and love—just as our hospice patients do. We had to say goodbye this week to my Daddy-O Dash. He was so loved and had the honor of his last retrieve. I know he is now running and playing and has found Callie and Max by now. My people are very sad, so I am spending some extra time loving on them.

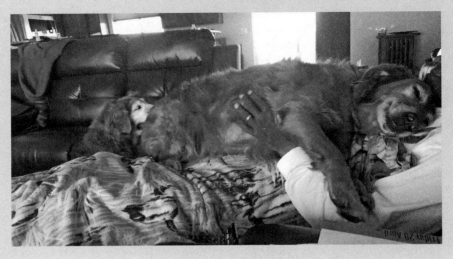

Without this goofy character Dash in my life, I would have never continued to pursue field games and I certainly would never have met a tall, dark, and handsome hubby. Nor would I have met all the amazing people I have in the past twelve years. Dash was not at all a good pick for me to start out with in hunt tests, but so it goes. He made some great puppies along the way, including JJ. It was a fantastic adventure. Until we see you again, Dash. Enjoy the never-ending supply of birds, bacon, and hot, girl dogs.

10

I fell in love with Golden Retrievers many, many years ago when I met the first dog who would partner with me in therapy dog work, Booker. I didn't know him as a puppy; I acquired him when he was a sweet, younger dog. When it was time to get another puppy, it was clear it would be another Golden. I had fallen in love with this fun, goofy, loving breed. Goldens are described as active, exuberant, inquisitive, busy, nosy dogs who have a naturally outgoing disposition and are devoted companions. They are good at whatever they do—be it hunting, serving as guide dogs, working search-and-rescue, or being devoted companions.

When a family member of an acquaintance had Golden puppies, I bought one, sight unseen, no clue what to be looking for other than the Golden part, and he was shipped to me in Seattle. When I got this Golden puppy, I learned what people meant by backyard breeders. This cute little male puppy arrived with a bacterial skin infection and two types of ticks, along with a potbelly from a multitude of worms. When I called the woman, she said, "Well, at least it's not fleas!" It took quite a bit of vet treatment to get him fixed up, and I used this lesson when I went looking for my next dog. Before getting Dash, I did a lot more research into what made a responsible breeder. I learned that each breed has specific health issues and there are different health clearances that apply, such as hip and eye clearances. These health clearances are used to decrease the likelihood of passing on hereditary conditions such as hip dysplasia or eye diseases. Over the years, more clearances have been added and there are now tests for some recessive genetic diseases as well. While there is no guarantee of avoiding health problems completely, performing the appropriate health clearances on the parents will significantly improve the odds of producing healthy puppies. Dash had been raised in the house and had been exposed to a lot of different stimuli growing up. He was a healthy, happy puppy and had the temperament to take on the world the minute he went home with me.

I have had many people ask me over the years why I don't go with a rescue dog for therapy work. Many, many dogs that have been rescued have made lovely companions and therapy dogs, while many others have had great hurdles to get through each day simply because of what they were exposed to prior to being rescued. You just never know what they will be like in many of the situations I encounter, and often, it takes a while to find out what ghosts they carry from that uncertain past. I commend all who put their love and energy into a dog who has not had the opportunity to share a loving and stable home. I love our Goldens and I have a significant influence over how they start their lives and which puppy will be the best fit for different families. I have knowledge of generations of temperament, health, and trainability information when deciding to have a litter of puppies. If we didn't breed occasionally, I would have never had JJ and been witness to the amazing connection she has with the people she meets. Our goal is to raise well balanced, stable, healthy, and happy puppies that grow up and spend their lives with people who love and care for them. We have not had our dogs show up in shelters—we stay in touch with most of the owners throughout the dogs' lives. No matter what they may do, whether it's therapy work, performance dog sports, field retrieving, Search and Rescue, or hiking and fishing partner, they are family companions first and foremost. For the most part, when it is time for us to get a new puppy, we select from one of our own litters.

I have been on an interesting adventure with dogs over the years. My goal has been to learn as much as I can about breeding, puppy development, and the enrichment it takes to give them the best start possible. We have evolved over time regarding how we raise litters and have had the input from very experienced people who have done this for a long time. Sometimes, my husband shakes his head at me since I often am adjusting our methods, but just like my hospice work, there is always something to be learned and applied.

The first thing that I learned was the need to have a tried and true plan to manage a group of intact dogs when a female has a heat cycle. We don't let our dogs outside unsupervised. Over the years, girls have always been housed and aired separately from the boys when someone was in heat and I swear, sometimes it seems like we should use big padlocks. Hormones run strong, determination is high, and I can see how it is easy for people to have unplanned pregnancies in their dogs if they aren't paying attention and being extra careful. Dash was always our early warning system, as he could detect a girl coming into heat a week ahead of time. He was always a whiny, crying hot mess of a stud dog when this occurred, though it was much worse toward the end of the heat cycle when the female ovulated. That sneaky Mother Nature knew what she was doing when it came to making sure animals reproduced. Dash would do his best to try to convince us of his undying love for whatever female was in heat at the time and would get annoyed to no end when we wouldn't oblige him. This kind of thing is not for the faint of heart or for the unprepared, as it goes on for three weeks or so. If allowed to, Dash would spend hours outside of his love's kennel run, doing his flirty dance and telling us all about it. I would look over at him and say, "Dash, it's not going to work out. She's a black Lab. Not your type. Sorry, Bud." If he could have thrown himself to the ground with his paw on his forehead just to dramatize the occasion more, he would have. Fun times.

When we decide to have a litter of puppies, we typically are going to keep one, and most are spoken for long before the breeding ever happens. When someone is interested in getting a puppy from us, we do our best to educate them about the breed characteristics to make sure a Golden puppy would be a good fit. Nothing breaks my heart more than hearing someone say they had to give up their dog because it was too big or too rambunctious—usually because they gave no consideration to what would happen beyond the "cute puppy" stage. All breeds are different and it's important for people to understand the breed's basic traits and characteristics, whether mixed or purebred, when bringing home a dog or puppy from a breeder or a shelter. A working breed with high energy such as a Border Collie, usually will not make a great couch potato. Dogs aren't something you grow out of. It's a commitment for the lifetime of the dog and cannot be a decision made on the spur of the moment.

All the dogs have always gone nuts when the warming basket comes out, signifying puppy time. They will continually poke their heads in it waiting for puppies to magically appear, especially JJ and Dash. They all know when a female is pregnant and when it is getting time for labor. In the typical "Hi, how are you this morning?" dog sniff greeting, there apparently is an "I'm good, puppy time soon," response back in the scent. They all act noticeably different and check in with her more frequently on the day before puppies arrive. Callie was always very helpful to have around when it was time for puppies. The dogs were often crated at night, but if we were expecting puppies, I would keep Callie out to free roam. While it would be so much easier on us if dogs would give birth during the daytime, most girls don't bother to read the "Having Your Puppies During Daylight Hours Makes for an Easier Labor" memo, so it usually is an all-night affair with popcorn and coffee at the ready. Callie had ears that could hear puppy squeaks from miles away, so I knew I could go to sleep if labor hadn't started. Once the first puppy arrived, she would come running to wake me up, "Timmy is down the well and the puppies are coming. Help!" JJ does the same thing and probably is even more intent on getting my attention than Callie ever was. Also, JJ is certain that every puppy born belongs to her. My husband and I take turns staying up all night if labor appears imminent. We have video cameras in the room so we can stay out of there, since it is best for an expectant mother to rest quietly. As tempting as it can be to fuss over any of the girls while they are in labor, Mother Nature knows her business and instinct kicks in very quickly once puppies start arriving. With the cameras, we can check on the progress without opening the door each time and know immediately if anything might be wrong based on the mom's behavior.

With our Labs and Goldens, we typically have litters that range from eight to twelve puppies. When there are only one or two, very often they have grown so big that the females have trouble giving birth. The term used for a dog giving birth is whelping, and it has normally, and fortunately, been uneventful for us. Puppy watch starts about one week ahead of the due date, when we check her temperature twice a day since a female's body temperature often drops dramatically twelve to twenty-four hours prior to giving birth. They will also usually refuse food prior to whelping, although this is not always the case. It would be very helpful if they all would follow the manual, but some like to keep us guessing. The whelping room is set up days ahead of time with all the supplies needed, including that warming basket the dogs are so fond of.

Young puppies are unable to regulate their body temperature and can die from being too cold. A cold puppy may nurse, but is unable to digest the food in its body and will slowly fade away. The room is temperature controlled so it doesn't get too cold or too hot, and we have a warming basket—containing a heating pad on one side set on low—in the room to keep puppies warm when they aren't in the whelping box with their mother. We use it when we have big litters and need to rotate puppies to make sure all are getting a chance to nurse. Even as newborns, some puppies can be little pigs. There is something called "nipple guarding," where a puppy falls asleep right next to where they were nursing and when another puppy comes in to root around, the first puppy will latch on quickly to keep the nipple to itself. Often, there is a disparity in size of pups, and it can be difficult for smaller puppies to fight to get enough to eat. When we rotate half of the puppies in and out of the warming basket every two hours, this ensures all get a fair turn at the milk bar. JJ loves when there are a lot of puppies, because she gets more time to be near them when they are being rotated.

TBO: "JJ, you have puppy on your breath."

Me: "Nuh-uh!"

TBO: "I know the smell of puppy. You reek of it!"

Me: "Mistaken identity. Frame job."

TBO: "I have a photo here. Whose hiney is this sticking out of the puppy basket?"

Me: "Rut roh."

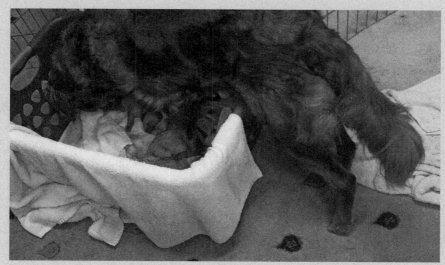

We know labor is progressing when the mother starts "nesting," literally shredding and digging to make a nice round nest. We use shredded newspaper for its absorbency during this process, and on camera you can see newspaper flying up left and right in the whelping box when she's at it. Left to their own devices, mother dogs would much prefer to build their own den outside where they would happily raise their puppies. It is quite common for them to be thinking this in the later weeks of pregnancy and they are industrious with their digging. The first year we moved in to our last house, Callie started digging a hole underneath the deck stairs. It apparently has a sign we couldn't see that said, "Puppy den here," because over the years all the mothers after Callie would work on this hole and try to convince us it was the place where all the cool moms were having puppies.

I'm not sure how anyone who whelps puppies without help does it, especially with larger litters. We are fortunate to have flexible schedules so that one of us can always be with the mother and then the puppies once they arrive. Our moms are pretty much on autopilot during the whelping process, but sometimes they do need help. We have had some puppies all arrive within three hours and some take twelve to twenty-four hours for all to make it into the world. It is common to have a couple born and then wait up to a couple of hours before more arrive. The waiting can be more than a bit nerve-wracking, even for those with a lot of experience. We check every puppy over, make sure their lungs are clear, that their cord is tied off and get a weight on them. Mom does most of the work unless she is too aggressive with biting the umbilical cord, and then we will step in. Each puppy gets a color-coded collar so we can tell them apart. Most of the time, our puppies all look like little, baked potatoes, with few distinguishing features to tell them apart, so the color coding helps us to monitor weights for the first week and keep track of who is getting rotated. Whelping a mess of puppies is hard work, and the moms typically sleep between contractions. Once all arrive, it is common for the females to take a very long nap. By this time, JJ is running around the house doing her best to convince us to let her see "her" puppies. I just want to sleep by this point, and she's ready to party.

Many people had asked me if JJ would ever have puppies. My husband and I had finally decided we would pursue one litter with her, after considering it for a long time. Since I wanted to become a certified Puppy Partner through Project Canine, I thought it would be a perfect combination to be screened while my therapy dog raised her litter. Like we do with all the breedings, we spent a lot of time researching pedigrees and traits of different males, determining who would be the best overall match. I was going to be keeping one of JJ's daughters and was hoping she would be able to follow in her mother's footsteps with therapy and crisis response work. You never really know, but it helps tremendously to start with two parents who have good temperaments and trainability. I couldn't imagine that JJ would have a puppy that didn't enjoy interacting with people the way she did, so my hopes were high. By the time we thought she was pregnant, we had done several HOPE AACR callouts (I'll explain more about this in another chapter), including Oso and Seattle Pacific University. Even though we don't name our litters as some breeders do, JJ's was different. I planned on this being the "Strong Litter" in honor of the resilient people JJ and I were honored to comfort as a Hope Animal-Assisted Crisis Response team. The hashtags #Osostrong and #SPUstrong were widely used after these tragic events. Each puppy in JJ's litter would have a name that meant "strong."

We were at SPU after the shooting for the HOPE AACR callout about two weeks after JJ was bred. She was easily fatigued and not eating as much as she normally would, but otherwise acted normally and still loved to interact with people. Since she didn't have a fever, the vet wasn't concerned at the time and cleared us to make our crisis response callout. Her behavior bothered me, but I just let her nap as much as she wanted. At thirty days post-breeding, we went in for the ultrasound to confirm pregnancy. Instead of seeing the tiny heartbeats of puppies, there was fluid instead. Blood work and the culture confirmed she had a closed pyometra, which is a uterine infection. My heart sunk. We were fortunate to catch it early, since many females die of this. While there are some that will try antibiotics and treatments to fix it, there was no question about having her spayed urgently. We simply were not willing to risk her life. The morning afterward, I woke up to an e-mail reporting that she did well through her operative day. However, at the end of the day when she was being taken outside, she tried to jump up on a table to get to some food. She had an incision with sutures, and jumping was not on her list of approved post-operative activities. I swear that dog's appetite will be her downfall. One of my co-workers said it best, "We love you JJ and are excited you will soon be back with us at work. I am so very thankful it was caught in time. So sorry you will not be a mommy, but you will continue to be an amazing nanny and our awesome therapy dog." At the time, it was overwhelmingly disappointing for the puppy owners who were waiting for this litter, myself included. "We just love JJ and we are so happy she is going to be OK. We know that she is a powerful, positive presence in the lives of so many. It's hard to let go of the future plans that we all were looking forward to. Fate has some strange things up its sleeve sometimes." I agreed with that, but it took some months to really sink in. In retrospect, it probably was for the best, as there is no way that the puppies would have been little clones of JJ, and I have the feeling some of the people interested in her puppies would have expected this. As another said, "Puppies would have been nice, but there is only one JJ and she cannot be risked; she has a lot of work ahead of her."

I'm off work for a few days while Ottie here is about to give birth, so I will be a MIDWIFE! Woo hoo!! I'm not totally sure of what this entails, but CrankyPants says wrestling and chewing on each other's face is NOT a part of it. Hmmppphhhhh. I thought I was doing so well in practice. I guess I need to do the Google and figure out what I am supposed to do.

Later that same year, we bred JJ's sister, Ottie, and decided to keep a puppy from this litter. I had the crazy notion to document one of the litters on social media, raising them "virtually" on JJ's page to show how much work and time goes into raising puppies responsibly. The puppies were Ottie's and came to be fondly known as The Littles. I knew I would get some grief along the way. In some circles, the climate has become very anti-breeder. I had some of my puppy owners feeling that they couldn't tell others they were getting a puppy because of the harassment they would receive. However, for the most part, the feedback I received was positive. People enjoyed seeing photos and videos as they grew and came to appreciate how much deliberate work goes into raising them correctly. We know that the crucial period for the socialization of puppies goes from three to twelve weeks, although if they have been raised a certain way, this period may very well extend to sixteen weeks. People seemed to love watching them grow over time, learning the ins and outs of puppyhood. I even heard from some who fostered puppies that they had started to incorporate some of the techniques of puppy rearing I was documenting. These methods are good for any puppy, so it was worth the time and effort it took to share and to answer people's questions.

The first two weeks of a puppy's life are a bit boring from the human perspective. If they aren't nursing, they are sleeping. Puppies are born with their eyes and ears sealed shut, getting by with noses that tell them where mama's milk is located. This is because when they are born, their nervous systems are still developing. At the beginning, female dogs nurse their puppies while lying down. As the puppies grow, mothers instinctually begin nursing from a sitting and then a standing position. This helps the puppies develop strength and coordination. As you can imagine, it is imperative to have a surface with good traction for the puppies so they do not slip. Along the way, I trim the puppies' nails every 5 to 7 days until they go home. Puppies instinctually knead when they are nursing to help express the milk. Long, sharp nails can injure a nursing female. When we have ten puppies, that's 160 nails each time and I've learned it is best done when they are sleeping. By the two-week mark, mothers are eating three to four times the amount of their usual food intake to keep up with milk production. Our puppies will start on their own puppy food by four to five weeks, but will continue to nurse if their mother will allow. For most of our litters, the puppies nurse for short periods until they go home, especially Ottie's litter. I swear she is a card-carrying member of the canine version of the La Leche

League. If left to her own devices, she would nurse her puppies and any others she could for as long as possible.

With our puppies, the eyes usually start opening around day twelve, after they have had a chance to fully form. During this period, as they get used to the light, we keep the whelping area darkened. A few days after this, their ears will open and they start the transition from little hamsters to full-fledged puppies. From days three through sixteen, we are deliberately handling them to help stimulate their neurological systems. We also perform Avidog's Early Scent Introduction as a way of stimulating the neurological system, specifically their sense of smell. A different scent is used each day. Examples are a leather glove, lavender sprig, lemon, feathers, a pine twig, tennis ball, and clove oil.

Once their ears open, the fun begins a few days later when they start the drunken sailor walk as they learn to use their legs. Not to be outdone, the puppy sushi stage is fun as well. Puppies are very orally fixated, exploring their world with their mouths, including their brothers and sisters. During this time, different noises are introduced to desensitize them to sounds they may encounter as they get older. Not only do we have TV and radio going at different times in the whelping room, we have a specific soundtrack we use. Noises include door knocking and doorbells, traffic, fireworks, household appliances, car engines, cat sounds, thunderstorms, and dog sounds. I usually leave the room for some of the soundtrack since I have heard it over and over and over. Puppies also get used to the standard household noises such as pots and pans banging together, the dishwasher and washing machine running—although with new high efficiency appliances, the sounds are not terribly impressive. We run the vacuum around the room, getting closer to them as they get older, eventually giving them treats next to it while it is running. I get feedback often about how our puppies are bold and curious when they go to their new homes, and I attribute it to all the work we do while they are growing. In Oregon, we don't get many thunderstorms, but recently we had some that caused quite a commotion. One of our owners reported how well her four-month-old puppy did. "She went outside, did her business and sat patiently by the door to come in. I have never had a pup not be scared during a thunderstorm. Now she is just sitting by the sliding door watching like it's no big deal. My kids, on the other hand, are in their couch fort until it passes."

Part of raising resilient puppies is giving them novel items and situations to deal with once they are three weeks old. As they develop, these things become more complex. Each day, something different is added to their area, such bubble wrap, a box with holes cut out of it, aluminum pie pans, a crinkle tunnel, paper towel rolls, different kinds of dog toys, an umbrella, a wobble board, a toddler slide, an empty dog food bag, and a skateboard. It is important when raising puppies not to bail them out of a challenging situation or make a huge fuss when something happens. We want them to face things that challenge, and even frustrate them, so they learn to work out a problem, rather than have an absolute fit or completely freak out and freeze. Coddling or rescuing all the time is not helpful down the road and doesn't prepare them for life's challenges. On the other hand, we watch to make sure they don't get too stressed out either. It's all about balance.

One of the best tools we have is an interactive activity station called an Adventure Box that allows us to introduce the puppies to sights, sounds, touch, and motion. This was developed by a company called Avidog, which was formed to bring the latest proven methods for raising puppies, with the goal that dogs will be as healthy, stable, and as well behaved as their genetics will allow. Avidog has free construction plans on their website, and Tellus built ours from those instructions. When the Adventure Box comes out, all the dogs love it. Dash would even lie in the middle of it as if it were a dog crate. The adults don't interact with it like the puppies do, but they know it's the place where all the action is going to happen. The puppy playroom gets very crowded when the nannies decide to join in. The Adventure Box is created out of PVC with all kinds of different things hanging from it including chain, small enamelware cups, a stiff plastic bristle brush, cut pieces of hose, soft mini paint rollers, clean metal cans and lids, plastic funnels, a small tire toy, and a rope toy. Some of the items are good for when they are four weeks old but must be changed out to more sturdy pieces by six weeks. Everything we introduce must be specific to their developmental period and be safe for them to play with. To keep the puppies stimulated, the Adventure Box comes in and out of their play area so they aren't too accustomed to it. By seven weeks, our monsters will do a quick job of deconstructing it, so it goes away at that point.

The other fun activity is to fill up a small pool with empty plastic bottles or balls when the puppies are about five weeks old. Puppies love to dive in, making all sorts of noise while playing King of the Pool. While it is fun to watch, along with everything else we do, there is a purpose behind the bottle pool. It helps to make the puppies very comfortable when stepping on things that move, hearing noises around them and having their bodies touched by non-living objects. Not only is it fun, it helps to build courage and overall confidence. All the things they are introduced to are designed to help grow stable, well-adjusted puppies who can adapt to new things and not be afraid of their shadows.

By three weeks, once the puppies can walk, we start introducing the litter tray for elimination. It is used to separate their bathroom area from their sleeping and eating areas, and gives puppy owners a head start on housetraining. When they are first introduced to the litter tray, it is placed just a few steps from their sleeping area. Since a puppy's bladder gets stronger over time, we can start moving the litter pan farther away. Eventually, by six to seven weeks, we have a 95% success rate. When they are in the play area, instead of just squatting, they will run to the box to go to the bathroom. Tellus laughed when I first told him I wanted to experiment with this type of tray training for the puppies, but then when I had to go out of town for a crisis response callout, leaving him with ten six-week-old puppies, he was amazed at how clean the puppy room stayed.

We are constantly handling and interacting with the puppies, especially once their eyes and ears open. They can be wild little monsters running around, but when we pick them up they just relax. Once they have their legs under them, cuddle time is done down on the floor to help prevent any jumping behavior. Puppies will try to put their paws up on people and if you pick them up, you reinforce good things will happen with that behavior. Be warned, an eight-week-old puppy can quickly train its owner in this regard before you even know what is happening. What is cute with a small puppy, is not at all charming, and can even be dangerous, with a fully grown dog. While it's tempting to ooh and aah at puppies while they are jumping up on their enclosure, this will set the stage for them to learn they can get a response while stretched up with their feet. We ignore that behavior and they only get praised and petted when they have "four on the floor." When I am standing in the puppy pen, the puppies get rewarded with a treat when they are waiting politely. Anytime one puts paws on me, I simply turn away and ignore them silently. This action is far more effective than verbally saying "no" over and over, especially with puppies. We become puppy treat Pez dispensers and reward the behaviors we want, such as coming to us when we call them while ignoring or redirecting away from behavior we don't want. Working the puppies with treats tends to bring the nannies running to show their skills. They know "four on the floor" as well, and fully expect to be rewarded for showing the puppies how big dogs do it.

Some people decide it would be fun to let their female dog have puppies without thinking through the commitment of what is involved. One reason people end up dumping young puppies, is they get very active by four weeks. That is when the work really begins, even for those who aren't doing all the enrichment activities we do. By five to six weeks they are eating a lot, which means the pooper-scooper gets a lot of action. It requires a lot of work to keep puppies fed, cleaned, and healthy. They are messy and get into everything if you don't have them set up properly. Depending on the breed, they do best when they can stay with their littermates for eight to twelve weeks. Larger breeds such as Goldens and Labs mature faster and ours do well when they go to their homes between eight and nine weeks. Part of a puppy's socialization is learning appropriate dog-to-dog interaction. If they are taken away from their littermates too early, they will miss out on crucial socialization skills. This often leads to many of the social and/or behavioral problems seen in older dogs. We are fortunate to have several trusted adult dogs that like being around puppies. Dash was known as the "manny" and loved his puppy time. He even could be found cleaning puppies at times, which is a bit unusual for a male. It is important to note that any time we allow adult dogs to spend time with the puppies, it is always supervised and only done if the mother is not stressed by the situation.

Bite inhibition is another reason it is important for puppies to stay with their mother and littermates. When nursing, if the puppy bites too hard, the milk bar gets up and walks away. Our females tend to keep nursing until it is time for puppies to go home, which helps to reinforce the lessons about biting. When working on bite inhibition, I want our puppies to be able to know how to mouth safely. Trying to do this by never letting them have their mouth on you is ineffective, especially with orally fixated Retriever puppies. There will be times when they may mouth you accidentally or you will have your fingers in their mouth when brushing teeth or doing mouth exams. They need to learn to cope with this and not bite down in these situations. I spend much of my time redirecting them with toys so they aren't learning to chew on me. We try not to let them chew on our pant legs, but puppies explore their world with their mouths and with so many of them, it can be challenging to manage. This is why Tellus gives me an incredulous look while shaking his head no and backing up if I ask him to go in with the puppies. He calls them piranhas and, unless I am working at the Hospice House, he leaves most of the puppy duties to me.

Playtime outside is important from four or five weeks on; it helps them become confident and curious explorers of their world. They are exposed to new things such as grass, rocks, dirt, sunshine, rain, and wind. We have things for them to climb onto to continue to stimulate their development, and they will follow their mother and nannies anywhere. We have yet to have a puppy that doesn't love to explore the great outdoors and they aren't shy about getting dirty. We used to have a fallen tree at our old house, which made a perfect play thing for the puppies to climb on and around. I tried to convince Tellus to bring it to our new property but was vetoed. People are always amazed that we can keep some semblance of order outside with all the puppies since it's like herding cats. I asked Tellus once how the puppies did with him while I was away from home, and he said, "Getting them out was a piece of cake. Getting them back inside, not so much! They scattered like a covey of quail. This is your job from now on." My secret weapon is Mom—they will follow the milk wagon anywhere, and I look like a rock star puppy trainer. When needed, I can get JJ to help as well, although she is easily distracted, which means they all head in a different direction.

I bet you didn't know I was part herding dog. When The Littles have a big walk and there are one or two who don't like the idea of coming back, I'm sent out. "JJ, find the puppies," and I'm on it! I go find the lost puppies and they follow me back. Oh wait. Squirrel!

Puppies have a couple of short fear periods—different breeds mature at different rates, so the fear periods occur at different times. Ours typically have it around four weeks and seven and a half weeks. During these fear periods, if the puppies are introduced to things in the wrong way, they can imprint as scary throughout their lives. Our puppies are typically very food motivated, so if they show any concern, treats rain down upon them for distraction. One thing that we like to do is make Therapy Puppy visits to the Hospice House before they go to their new homes, but I schedule visits before and after their second fear period. Our goal is to have confident, bold puppies that easily transition to their new homes. The owners then continue the socialization we have done for the past five weeks.

When people ask me if I get sad when the puppies go home, I can honestly say no. They have great homes to go to, and by eight and a half weeks, many are sporting small war wounds from beating each other up. We are exhausted from all the work, and it typically takes several days to make the house presentable again, since housework goes on the back burner for the majority of puppy time. Even the mothers and the nannies move on to gopher hunting and long naps once all have left. Our girls don't get depressed once puppies leave, but some of that may be because we have so many other dogs for them to play with.

When I shared the experience with the litter with so many people on the puppy page, I never anticipated the strong bond so many would develop with puppies they had never met. While I was happy to have the little monsters move on to their new homes, many people were very sad they wouldn't be seeing posts about them anymore. The feedback I got was tremendous and I found out how even a virtual puppy could help provide comfort and happiness to those around the world. More than a few people sent me messages about how the puppy posts got them through some very dark times.

> "I have smiled, laughed out loud, cried, and been touched so deeply from what transpires on this page. I am so grateful a friend would share the posts so that I, too, could enjoy the Littles even though they were almost ready to move on. I am in awe and inspired by what Tracy does, and still takes the time to share the joys and pains of her work. I am so grateful to be a part of this experience!"

"The last several weeks have been amazing and educational. Thank you! We got to experience the magic of puppies without accidents or whining. You and the crew are most appreciated!"

"Thanks for creating such a wonderful place on Facebook. I loved watching the puppies after a stressful day at work. You truly provide a community service to your followers."

"I don't know if you truly know how much joy you bring people. I've been recovering from surgery for the past three weeks, and these pictures are everything. Thank you so much."

"Following the saga of the Littles was one of the most educational, delightful and heartwarming experiences I've ever had on Facebook."

"This page makes me happy, as I am a cancer patient. I love the Littles, I love JJ, I love it all! It's therapy for me."

It wasn't until one of the puppyies' owners relayed a story to me that I realized just how popular the virtual puppies had been. As a young puppy, Cleo would visit her owner's family in a nursing facility some miles away. When they first walked into the facility, the staff knew exactly who she was at first glance. Her owner was told they all follow JJ's page and recognized her the moment she walked in.

There is a downside to having such famous puppies, and it came to all of us unexpectedly. Some of the puppy owners had created Instagram accounts, and each quickly had several hundred followers. Two of Ottie's girls, Cleo and Lily, were placed in local homes, which is unusual for us. One of these families was on the list for a later litter, but due to a cancellation, we were able to tell them they could have a puppy out of this litter. I could see both Cleo and Lily frequently, especially since one of Lily's owners is a Hospice House volunteer. Not only was Lily—the puppy known as Piggy Pink because she wore a pink collar and could be counted on to nipple guard—extremely well-known on social media, all the hospice staff and volunteers knew her as well, so her visits were always a hit. She was the puppy with the sweet demeanor who loved to get belly rubs and just be around people. On her first camping trip with her owners, she got to meet many people. While her owners were talking to a group of women, Lily was enjoying spending time with them, even resting her head on one woman's lap. In a sign of what a small world it can be: when they mentioned they were hoping Lily would become a therapy dog, one of the women said she knew of one at a Hospice House in Albany.

When Lily was about seven weeks old, we noticed she had some roundness to her skull, but at her vet visit, I was told not to be concerned. On her subsequent puppy wellness exams after she went home, nothing was mentioned about her head shape, other than it was a little different.

At four and a half months, she came back to stay with us while her people went camping at a location that wasn't deemed safe for a pup. She spent the first couple of days back with us running and playing with JJ, Gamine, and her mother Ottie. During the day and at night, she bunked with her mother and had a lot of snuggle time. Early one afternoon, as I went to take them outside again, I noticed something was very wrong. Lily couldn't come out to greet me and when I picked her up and set her on the ground, she had great difficulty walking. I could guess that the problem was neurological and sped off to the emergency vet. In the short trip to get there, she had declined even more. As a hospice nurse, it doesn't take much for me to recognize a life slipping away, human or canine. I was panicked trying to reach her owners, who were out of cell range, but no matter what, we would do whatever Lily needed. I wasn't prepared for the vet's initial assessment, but in retrospect, it all makes sense. "I'm worried about hydro-cephalus with the shape of her head and her neurological impairment." There was no way to definitively diagnose this without an MRI, but for us it was a moot point. She was no longer even tracking with her eyes as I sat on the floor with her, willing for this all to be one awful nightmare I would wake up from. She was admitted and given supportive care until we could reach her owners, although I was prepared to make the decision myself to let her go that night if needed. When I left her at the hospital, she no longer responded or even indicated she knew I was there.

Looking back, we all recognized that Lily's time on earth would be short regardless of if we had known the diagnosis or not. A fluke congen-ital defect that is rarely seen in Goldens was never even on my radar. As breeders, we all understand that you never know what happens when DNA combines, just as when birth defects happen in children. While it has been a very hard time, we all agree that for whatever reasons, the fates knew what exactly what they were doing with this special puppy. She was deeply loved by her people and ended up in the best possible home. She got to play with her nanny JJ and snuggle with her mother right up to the end. Her short time on earth meant so much to so many and she will not be forgotten. Grieving in public can be much more difficult than grieving privately. Lily's owners asked me to share the news on social media for them. I appreciate that so many love the dogs, but there is also a weight in having an animal that is so beloved by many, especially at the time of loss.

We have had many puppies over the years, and we love when owners stay in touch and share special stories. The litter I remember as the most fun was one that we never had intended to breed. We had a person who had a deposit on a future litter from Callie for Search and Rescue work. When Callie was diagnosed with cancer, we knew she would not have any more puppies, even if she were to survive her cancer. Gamine was getting older but had done so well as a mother, that we decided to do one last breeding, though, due to her age, we expected we wouldn't have many puppies. We ended up with the Three Amigos, and I had a blast with them. Gamine did very well, proving she could be a stellar mom even at an older age. As Tellus pointed out, "Only Gamine could GAIN weight when nursing." There was only one boy, and he would be named Dingle and was earmarked to train to become a Search and Rescue (SAR) dog. At the time Dingle was born, I didn't know the concept of Early Scent Introduction, but I was provided with the latest research in SAR, which indicated we had a specific window of opportunity to introduce him to scent to help with his training as he got older. Often in training dogs for human remains detection work, they will use small pieces of donated human placenta. His owner arranged to come to the house for this specific scent introduction when Dingle was three weeks old. Since I'm a nurse, there isn't much that bothers me. Hubby, on the other hand, took off like he had a fire lit under him. I still laugh about it today, especially since it was only the scent on a Q-tip. He acted like we were going to whip out a big chunk of tissue right there in the living room.

It has been fun to live vicariously through Dingle's adventures in becoming a Search and Rescue dog and watch his ongoing training. He is certified in Wilderness Air Scent and human remains detection. As a puppy, he always was the adventuring type. If he disappeared, it was an interesting scavenger hunt to find him in the house. Not only has he had training in underwater scent detection, he has had the opportunity to train on rubble piles typically associated with disasters, and to practice getting in a helicopter and riding on horseback.

One of Shylah's littermates, Mac Duff, was selected to go into a service dog program, Paw Pals Assistance Dogs. He is working toward becoming a full-service wheelchair assistant and has been in training, socializing, and experiencing worldly sights and sounds with his puppy raiser since he was around eight weeks of age. He is finishing his advanced training and is now learning how to retrieve directed items, pull open and close doors, and be a great assistant. During the time when he was with his first puppy raiser, she sent me a very sweet story: "I just wanted to give you an update on Mac Duff. Last week I took him to work and was checking e-mail, when I learned a co-worker's donated kidney was failing. She has had this donated kidney for twelve years. I went down the hallway and there was another person in her office. Mac Duff did not care and he could not get to her fast enough. She stood up, sat on the floor, and Mac Duff just melted in her arms and would not leave her. Every time she stopped petting him, he just put his nose under her hand. When we left, he went back into my office and slept for a while. He also will do anything for a child. Thank you for Mac Duff. I love him so much, but I know he has a job to do for someone else." This story reminds me of the connection JJ has with others who need her on a regular basis. I have a feeling Mac Duff will do great things in the world, and I thank his puppy raising family for all the work they did with him.

Ottie's daughter, Cleo, has shown some amazing intuitiveness at a very young age. Her owner relayed to me that the nine-week-old puppy had only been living with them for all of five days when, "Cleo did something that surprised me last night, considering she's so young. My young daughter had some bad coughing episodes last night due to a cold. Every time she coughed, Cleo would start whining. I thought maybe the sound scared her. But the couple of the times I took her outside to go to the bathroom, she would whine unless I took her with me to Sophia's room. Eventually, I took Cleo and my daughter downstairs with me. We camped out in the living room so everyone else could sleep. Cleo slept right next to Sophia on the couch. This morning she won't leave Sophia's side. As I type this, they are both on the couch watching a Disney movie, and every time Sophia coughs, Cleo licks her hand." Before she was six months old, Cleo showed how in tune she was with her owner. "I don't know what I'd do without my little Monster. My doctor started me on a new medication, and I've been having some dizzy spells while I adjust to it. This afternoon was bad. She has stuck to me like glue and laid on me when a bad spell hit and she won't let me get up." Cleo may become a therapy dog when she is older, but she obviously is doing important work for her family members already.

As a breeder, Teej was one of my heart puppies. He was dark yellow, one of twelve black and yellow Lab puppies born in 2007, and his was the first litter Callie ever took over as nanny extraordinaire when we were living in California. One of Teej's owners was diagnosed with cancer shortly before the puppies were due to go home. She was facing cancer treatment, including surgery, and we spent quite a bit of time trying to figure out if it was even feasible for her to try to raise a puppy at that time in life—a young, energetic puppy is not easy to care for post-op. On the other hand, when facing something as daunting as cancer, maybe he would be exactly the medicine she needed. After discussions with her surgeon and oncologist about the possibility of raising a puppy during her time of treatment, the decision was made for Teej to go home with them. The story of his beginning with his family, not knowing what was in store for the future, and then the amazing news of her remission and then her first pregnancy still brings tears to my eyes. Teej has not only been able to help raise two boys, but he also became a therapy dog who helped other children along the way, long after he helped his mom get through her cancer.

Callie's first nanny job was Teej and his siblings, and here is Teej on his first nannying job with his brother.

Teej's family has many touching stories over the years, but one story stands out as a testament to the power of the human-animal connection. Teej and his owner were volunteering as a part of A Fair Shake for Youth program based in New York City, which is designed to help young people build empathy, self-esteem, and develop tolerance and patience in some of the most impoverished and underserved communities in the city. They do this by using therapy dog teams paired with groups of middle schoolers in the program over a ten-week period. When the students are doing things like giving the dogs basic obedience commands and teaching tricks, they learn the value of communication and learning together. They see how building a trusting relationship gets results with the dogs and can be applied to their lives outside the program. They learn about shelters, rescues, and breed discrimination in dogs, based on the assumption that all dogs of a certain breed are dangerous without getting to know the individual dog. For these kids, most are all too familiar with being labeled simply due to their circumstances, over which they have no control. I got the story later from Teej's owner, when she shared with me this touching letter of a memorable connection between Teej and one student.

"I am a teacher in the South Bronx and I supervise the students who attend A Fair Shake sessions each term. It's always amazing to watch the middle schoolers connect with the dogs. But there is one connection during the 2015 winter session that was amazing and unforgettable.

The session started in January, in the middle of a particularly brutal winter. The students, as always, were very excited about working with the three therapy dog teams that would be coming every week. One student, an eighth-grade girl—whom I'll call Alice—had agreed to do the program but was terrified of dogs. She never said why and I didn't ask. I always attend the sessions, but I sit off to the side. Alice decided she would sit with me, far away from the dogs so she would be safe.

The Fair Shake teacher, the dogs, and the handlers enthusiastically began the lessons. The students worked hands-on with the dogs. They learned the safe way to greet new dogs and the importance of positive reinforcement when training basic obedience, tricks, and agility. They discovered that dogs communicate primarily through body language, and how the dogs get to know each other and people through scent. They participated in discussions about working dogs, shelters, puppy mills, and breed discrimination.

Through it all, Alice sat quietly at my side. In the beginning, her body language was closed and guarded. It was hard to read her. Her facial expression was without affect. She didn't participate, but she was watching and listening. And she had her eye on one dog. An eight-year-old, oversized, wonderfully goofy Labrador Retriever named Teej.

Teej loved the classes and the kids. When offered a belly rub, Teej would roll onto his back and put his head on the student's lap. His upside down, floppy jowls, flecked with grey, actually seemed to grin. At times, he would give voice to his joy with what sounded like a throaty yodel. I noticed Alice smiled each time he did this.

We were at the end of the winter session. It was the very last class when Alice made a surprising move. At the beginning of class, she joined the circle of students who were with Teej. She tentatively reached out and petted him. Teej reacted as if he finally had the attention of the human he'd longed for his entire life. He inched his way closer to Alice, rolled on his belly and plopped his big ol' head in her lap. Alice did not flinch. She smiled and kept right on petting him.

Teej and Alice stayed together for the rest of that class. Watching them, you'd swear they'd been together forever. Alice never stopped smiling. Teej was in dog heaven with his new friend. This amazing connection between a dog and a child is what makes our program and its dogs such an important part of our curriculum. Teej did something wonderful for Alice, a child who lives in a world of risk, struggle, neglect, and fear. He gave her his full attention, his unmitigated joy, and his love."

Teej is approaching ten years old and I still love to see the photos of him with his human brothers. He is still that dark yellow dog, but now has a white sugar face. As his owner and I recently reminisced about their life with Teej, her words melted my heart.

"I just have to tell you that everybody who meets Teej loves him. They all notice how sweet, sensitive, loving, and nurturing he is. I know I'm his mom, but he truly is an amazing dog.

I know for some people this is hard to comprehend, but he

really did save my life. He was the one ray of light when I truly was in the darkest place in my life. He made me get up in the morning. He gave me a purpose. He NEEDED ME to take care of HIM. It wasn't about me being sick; it was about us taking care of each other. I couldn't stay on the couch riddled with chemicals and utterly exhausted from throwing up, so close to the edge of falling into depression. Of course, it would be excusable. And didn't I have the right? Yes, but there was a little fox red puppy with the largest paws weighing him down, staring at me saying, 'Come on, Mom. Get up. We gotta go out and play and I need to pee pretty bad, by the way.' So, I got up. I moved forward. One day at a time. And he was honestly the reason.

And now, when I see him do this for others, who may be not facing a life or death diagnosis but are faced with pretty significant challenges, it makes me so happy. I see him lift them up, bring them joy, and give them love. I try to hold my tears to the end of our volunteer sessions, when I'm sitting in the car on the way back home.

I am overcome with gratitude that you and Tellus gave me one of the best gifts of not only my life but to so many more kids who are struggling with very real physical, social and emotional challenges. Thank you. From the bottom of my heart, thank you."

11

Our therapy dog organization, Project Canine, has a unique program for certifying puppies for therapy visits. It was developed because of the belief that Animal-Assisted Therapy visits with puppies are good for people, and—of equal importance—socializing with different people is good for puppies. But it is challenging to find a puppy who is capable of certifying at such a young age. Most of the time, it is best to work on socialization, play, and obedience training long before it is time to continue on to therapy work. Puppies grow very quickly and I always encourage people to focus on enjoying this period, as it goes by so quickly.

In addition to having the option of certifying qualified puppies, Project Canine's Puppy Partnership was developed for reputable, humane breeders, puppy raisers, and other canine professionals like trainers and behaviorists who might need to work with multiple puppies over the course of the certification period. When we decided to breed JJ, I was not only excited to have a daughter of hers, but also to use the opportunity to become Project Canine's Puppy Partner. For this credential, it is the handler who is tested and certified rather than a specific puppy. Before someone can gain this endorsement, the handler is required to take a written exam covering early puppy behavior, development, health concerns, socialization, and humane training. The handler must also demonstrate safe handling of puppies six weeks to five months in a hands-on demonstration, and references from two clients and a veterinarian are required. Once the handler has passed the exam, they are insured to visit with any puppy in their care until the puppy is five months old.

When I was unable to use JJ's puppies to earn my Puppy Partnership endorsement, I had the opportunity to do so with Ottie's litter. I knew I would be keeping one of JJ's nieces from this litter and would be able to continue our puppy visits once her littermates went to their new homes. Our Project Canine Oregon coordinator had the job of coming over to interact with the litter and videotape them for our certification. Part of the certification process involves a tour of the environment where the puppies are conceived, whelped, raised, and socialized by an approved Project Canine Instructor/Examiner or Board member with the appropriate background. As with any of our Project Canine certifications, this one is good for two years and then I will need to go through the same process to recertify. I know she is thinking "Oh darn! I have to go play with puppies AGAIN?"

In the spirit of what would have been JJ's litter, I chose the name Shylah for the puppy I kept. It is an Irish name that means strong. People often have asked me how I pick the puppy I feel will be a good fit down the road for the volunteering we do, and it isn't always easy. I kept a female from an earlier litter with the same goal of eventually doing therapy work, and she was one of those puppies who didn't have the heart of a lion, but she was extremely sweet and very people oriented. Once she was four months old, it became clear that she was a bit too timid for me and would be a better fit in another situation, so we placed her with the family of a medically fragile young child who needed a calm puppy. She has thrived in her home and has the perfect temperament for this family's needs. That experience taught me a bit more about what characteristics to look for in a puppy for my own needs. Shylah was bold, adventurous, sassy, and very attentive as a puppy, as were many of the puppies from her litter. I needed a confident and curious puppy to start this process with. We hope Shylah will make a good Project Canine therapy dog and maybe eventually a Hope Animal-Assisted Crisis Response K-9, but only time will tell as she grows older.

Once I was a Puppy Partner, I could take our puppies to our Hospice House for visits when they were between seven and eight weeks old. These are the perfect kinds of visits that help in the socialization of puppies before they go to their new homes. It is beneficial to be exposed to a new place, with unique sights, sounds, and smells, along with a host of people very eager to spend time with puppies. Shylah and her brothers Ben and Mac

Duff were the first ones to make Project Canine Puppy Partner visits at the Hospice House. Shylah had already earned the nickname "The Twerp" and I was determined to give her the best foundation I could in those first few months.

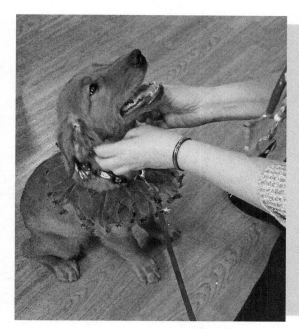

Well, the Twerp was a huge hit today. Everyone was impressed by how calm she was. She didn't mouth anyone, sat nicely when asked, and didn't get over-whelmed by all the sights and smells. She rocked the unexpected fire alarm, barely even reacting to the loud noises. Now she's back home, has shed her Super Puppy cape and is back to being wild and crazy.

Shylah's brother Ben was timid, unlike his self-assured sister, so I spent extra time with him for the extra two weeks he stayed with us. We had identified his shyness at five weeks old, and my husband and I both had worked with him individually to help him gain some confidence in unknown environments. The visits to the Hospice House were helpful for him to learn to be in new places and meet even more new people while building up some courage. I took JJ along on each of his visits to help him feel comfortable and to role model for him. He liked people and there were plenty of volunteers who were willing to cuddle with him, and it didn't hurt that he was treat-motivated, which helped get him through times that were scary for him. Mac Duff, a future service dog, stayed with us an extra few days before he flew off to be with his puppy raiser. He enjoyed making the puppy visits and seemed very secure. Miss Shylah had a confident atti-tude the moment we walked into the building. Everyone took notice of the bounce in her step and her demonstrations of a polite sit. It reminded me a bit of the way Taz commanded attention as a tiny kitten when I first took him home. Between the three puppies, it was an hour worth of visiting with staff and visitors who really appreciated it. I got one message that said, "You just erased 48 hours of awful stress for me!" For raw material in the hopes of having a future therapy and/or crisis work partner, I was very pleased with the puppy I had finally chosen. I was also thankful to have the opportunity to be able to start her socialization and training so early due to the Puppy Partnership program.

It's been a couple of busy days since I escorted The Littles to make some therapy puppy visits at the Hospice House. I helped show them the way, and I just might have been a WEE bit jealous of all the attention they were getting. We did have to check pockets before leaving to make sure everyone was accounted for.

Shylah was the first puppy I had raised beyond nine weeks since JJ. I mixed short training sessions with plenty of playtime, especially after Ben went home. I thought we'd settle into a nice routine, but two days later the little spitfire Taz showed up. Even though it was very nutty and chaotic for a few days, it turns out a curious little kitten makes for an excellent distraction while doing puppy training. I spent time working Shylah on obedience commands while Taz ran amok through our training sessions. Shylah handled it like a champ, although I did have to use food often to reinforce my commands. The videos of these training sessions still make me giggle to this day. Even if she doesn't go on to be a therapy dog as an adult, the foundation work done as a puppy helps to ensure that she will be a good citizen and companion.

I was much more deliberate with Shylah's early puppy training than I was with JJ's. With each puppy comes new learning and the knowledge to apply lessons I missed with previous dogs. When this young, obedience and good manners are a place to start, along with socializing, socializing, and more socializing. JJ missed out on tall men with hats and alien space creatures (riders with helmets) on motorcycles coming up behind the car—those people still give her fits. With Shylah, I was always keeping my eye open for novel situations to introduce her to. Puppies are a lot of work, but the effort put in very early on creates the building blocks for a stable, well-rounded dog who can handle life with his or her people. This goes for all dogs. The time you put in helps to create a relationship with your dog, and as in all relationships, the effort you spend over time continuing to build that relationship makes the bond stronger.

Okay, for those of you following The Twerp as she grows up, this was today's lesson. It is an important lesson for dogs, therapy or not, to be polite and not bolt through doors. The rumors of me doing remedial work on this now with the pack are completely unsubstantiated (and not on video, so there!).

As a puppy, Shylah made visits to the Hospice House, a memory care facility, and our local hospital—until she was five months old, the Hospice House visits took place weekly. I recall a funny moment with the children, a toddler, and a three-and-a-half-year-old daughter, in a young family that was staying at the Hospice House for several days. JJ and I had been working a long stretch and had spent a lot of time with them, so I decided to take Shylah in on my day off to see them too. The older sister remembered meeting JJ on Thanksgiving, but she was completely baffled when we walked in. She looked at Shylah and said, "How did she shrink?" All the adults around her smiled and laughed, breaking the tension of a really sad time for them. Just a short visit of twenty minutes with a puppy made a huge difference for staff, volunteers, and visitors. While everyone loves spending time with JJ, there is just something magical about puppy love, especially when people are stressed out or sad. I have found I need to plan the Puppy Partner visits well in advance because the staff wants to schedule time in their day to be at the Hospice House to see puppies. It is an absolute highlight for everyone.

I continued to work on Shylah's obedience training and got her used to being bathed and groomed, something every therapy dog needs to tolerate.

I use a grinding tool for their nails, to keep them short and smooth. Shylah was introduced to this vibrating sensation at six weeks old and like the rest of the dogs, she is very tolerant. I never get over how all our dogs will swim in a pond until forced to get out, but if they are subjected to a bath, it apparently is the end of the world. If JJ had her way, all baths would be conducted in a pond with a good roll around the grass and dirt to dry off. We have yet to see eye-to-eye on this matter. She doesn't even appreciate her special bath towel, Cookie Monster.

Look who's graduated to the Cookie Monster. She can have him, no good comes from Cookie Monster making an appearance. The Twerp is doing a visit today, standing in for me at our memory care unit.

Recently, I was contacted about making a hospital visit, as a physician had written an order for a therapy dog visit for a patient. Our smaller local hospital does not have therapy dog teams who visit regularly, but many in our system know of the therapy dogs at the Hospice House. We were working that day, but were able to get one of our on-call nurses to visit with her young Cardigan Corgi, Phoebe. Phoebe is a Project Canine certified therapy dog, who happened to also be our first certified Therapy Puppy in Oregon. With one blue eye, one brown eye, and her perky large ears, she is stunning to look at and everyone enjoyed her visit. The next day, I decided to take Shylah in for another ordered visit instead of JJ. At the time, she was three and a half months old, rocking a Christmas collar, and she did well for her first time in a hospital. Everyone loved meeting her, including the patient we were asked to see and the doctor who wrote the order. There really is something extraordinary when a puppy is interacting with people and clearly enjoys it. It made me very thankful and proud of her.

My husband and I have ongoing discussions about whom Shylah belongs to. When JJ was young, I was the one who did all her training and she was with me all the time. In retrospect, that probably wasn't the greatest idea. She is great with him when I am not around, but if I am nearby and he gives her a command, she looks at him as if to say, "Nuh-uh! You're not my mommy. You can't tell me what to do. I'm not listening. MOM!" This is a common occurrence when one member of the family focuses on doing the training with a dog. They learn to take commands from just one person. JJ absolutely loves Tellus, but in her mind, she doesn't have to obey him if I am around. We had decided to have Shylah spend time with both of us training, especially since she showed aptitude and interest in retrieving at a young age.

By five months, she had made enough therapy puppy visits to earn her AKC Therapy Dog Novice title. Once she turned six months and could no longer make visits under my Puppy Partnership liability, she started on her field training with Tellus full time. While she spent most of her training time with him from six months to eighteen months, I would take her out periodically for people time. She has an incredibly high drive for retrieving, but she also has a nice "off" switch when out visiting. She is calm and focused and is a pleasure to be around. She also will listen to both of us, so our training strategy appears to have worked. As usual, I may be the softie, but she absolutely adores my husband, as do all the dogs.

Woot, woot! The Twerp got called up from the minor leagues today and got to go on her own shopping trip at Wags Dog Emporium. It was a great training adventure with staff who are very dog savvy and they even helped with some of her training. There was a little boy who just couldn't get enough of her, though I need to have a talk with her about all those darned kisses.

Shylah has the best of both worlds. She gets to have fun out in the field, running and retrieving to her heart's desire, while maintaining her love of interacting with people and following in her aunt's footsteps. It will be fun to watch her mature over the years.

12

In 2009, I signed up for volunteer training with a group that provides emotional support for those who have been traumatized during some kind of emergency. It was an extensive training program on how to provide emotional first aid and practical support for those affected. Volunteers are on call twenty-four hours a day and respond when asked by emergency responders following events such as unexpected deaths, crimes, and emergency scenes after house fires, community disasters, and traumatic motor vehicle accidents. I couldn't help but think what a good fit a therapy dog might be during some of these situations, as the goal is to provide compassionate support for victims. Just before I was going to finish this training, my mother was diagnosed with ALS and all my extracurricular activities came to a halt. By the time I was ready to pursue this volunteer work again, I discovered the local chapter had folded because of a lack of funding.

After JJ and I had been doing therapy work for a while, I decided to pursue this interest again. Oh, the powers of an Internet search! To my great excitement, I discovered HOPE Animal-Assisted Crisis Response. They have been in existence since 2001, so obviously I was not the first to consider using a dog as a part of a volunteer team helping during traumatic events. I submitted an inquiry, got some information, and decided this could be a great way to give back to our community. The HOPE dogs provide comfort and encouragement through animal-assisted support for people affected by crises or disasters, which was exactly what I was looking for in my volunteer work. Those who consider joining must currently be a registered member of a formal animal-assisted therapy organization and have made at least a dozen volunteer visits. Handlers must be at least eighteen years old, and their canine partner must be at least eighteen months old. Check, check, and check. I talked with my husband about it and decided to start the process with JJ as my canine partner.

The first step was to watch an informational Open House webinar. This gives prospective members a comprehensive overview of HOPE AACR and lets them decide if they want to pursue going through the certification process. As I watched it, I just kept thinking "THIS! This is what I had in mind a few years ago. Sign us up." HOPE AACR also has team leaders, who work without a dog to supervise and support canine teams. It is a great role for those who still want to do this volunteer work, but do not have a canine partner.

Following the Open House, our next step was going to the screening evaluation. These are designed to help qualify handlers and dogs for certification training. A screening consists of an in-depth interview, interactions with HOPE evaluators, obedience skills test, crate test, and a role-play scenario designed to test for crisis response aptitude. Individuals without dogs go through a similar screening process and are evaluated on their leadership skills and aptitude for assisting canine crisis response teams. I was a bit nervous when we arrived for our screening, just because I wasn't sure exactly what to expect other than it would take three to four hours to complete. JJ gets easily bored when people are talking around her and aren't giving her attention, so she just settled and went to sleep while I answered questions from the HOPE member who was interviewing me. After the interview, the screener interacted with JJ and checked her over in the same way that is done during our therapy dog evaluations. We had to demonstrate basic obedience, as well as have a supervised separation period. I left JJ with my screener and went out of the room for five minutes with the other handlers. In a crisis response deployment, there could be a time when I might need to leave JJ with a team leader for a short time and this helps to make sure the dogs can handle this without undue stress. Like all the other dogs, she handled it well but kept a close eye on the door I used to exit and was happy to see me walk back in. As handlers, we were evaluated the entire time, even during breaks. It was important for the screeners to know we would continue to attend to our dogs at all times. The dogs needed to behave with food out on a table and other dogs milling around, they had to demonstrate they could be crated for several minutes, another thing that might be necessary during a deployment. JJ was crate trained as a young puppy for a variety of reasons and spent the time napping, highly unimpressed with this part of the evaluation.

It was going well until our shelter scenario. I tried to get up into the lap of a woman who was "afraid of dogs." Those people didn't know what they were talking about though. She was a dog person; I could smell them all over her! I ignored all the loud noises except for the crying babies, and I was quite certain I needed to find them. So much for me being different than my nanny Callie when it comes to babies. OOPS.

The biggest part of the screening evaluation is the role-play scenarios. These occur in a simulated shelter and all teams spend time with different people. We as handlers were all nervous about this part. During our screening, I remember one person was hysterical, one was afraid of dogs, and one person was very withdrawn. Some scenarios only had us interacting with one person, while there were two or three people in others. I might add our volunteers for these were very committed to their roles. Our screening did have one person who was going through as a team leader, so she took the lead to help all the teams get to the shelter and engage with the people in these scenarios. To really make this a true to life chaotic situation, there was a soundtrack playing during the scenarios with sirens blaring, babies crying, and the sounds of general chaos. I noticed JJ was most distracted when she heard babies crying loudly in the background. I made note to do some more desensitization exercises with her after this. We were challenged to try to engage the people in the shelter in an appropriate manner depending on how they were reacting to us. It's safe to say we bombed a bit when it came to dealing with the person afraid of dogs. In hindsight, I would have given more space to the person, as well as make sure I had my hand on her chest to make sure she didn't give an unwelcomed hug. I think it's safe to say the dogs all handled the stress far better than the handlers did during this exercise. It's normal for anyone to be nervous and try just a little too hard to do the exercises "right." Luckily, for those teams who show the aptitude for crisis response work, there is a lot of specific training that happens during the certification workshop to get us ready for actual callouts. All members of my screening group were invited to go on to the certification workshop held that year in Bozeman, Montana, including Casey, a Dalmatian who also has many jobs like JJ does.

It was clear to me after watching the webinar and participating in the screening evaluation that the crisis response dogs are much more than a basic therapy dog. My original thought all those years ago about having a therapy dog along to comfort people was a simple, naive one without the understanding of the complexity a canine partner adds. So much goes into the training of both dog and handler, and I was looking forward to getting that education once we arrived at the workshop. There are many therapy dogs and handlers who may do great at the shorter therapy dog visits but would be above their heads trying to transition to the much more stressful role as a crisis response team. While a regular therapy dog visit is done in a familiar environment for maybe an hour once every other week, crisis callouts usually span up to a four-hour block of time with assignments over one to three days in an unfamiliar environment. It is very tiring for handlers and dogs at the end of those visits. Imagine interacting with fifty to one hundred or more people over a few hours. Many of these callouts involve very intense emotions as well.

We were told some of the things to expect during our certification workshop, and being an overachiever, I decided more desensitization exercises were needed with JJ before the weekend of the workshop. I started using the soundtrack I use with puppies to get them used to sounds like thunder, traffic, vacuum, fireworks, dogs barking, and the ever-popular babies crying. I would play the soundtrack for short periods of time while we were driving, especially the baby section—I wanted to get JJ to the point where she could tune out the crying for the most part. I must say, while she got used to these noises, the crying babies about put me over the edge. Apparently, my personal desensitization was an epic fail; I was happy when we could move onto other things.

The location for the workshop in Montana was at Eagle Mount Center, an amazing facility that works with those who are disabled, as well as kids affected by cancer. Therapeutic horseback riding is a big component, and I realized JJ had never been around any large farm animals, including horses. Luckily, our hospice medical director has horses and we could visit just to get her familiar with them. She wasn't overly reactive but was fascinated by them, including the curious young colt and the burro.

One of the field trips during the certification workshop is a visit to a fire station. This was another thing that certainly was not on my list of "must visits" when JJ was a puppy. I figured it couldn't hurt to make a stop ahead of time to at least expose her to some of the sights, sounds, and smells, especially since she still got concerned any time she saw tall men in hats. The husband of one of my co-workers is stationed at a local fire station, and I arranged visits at two separate stations. When we arrived at the second fire station, many of the firefighters had just returned from assisting with fires in another part of the state, so the turnout gear room was full of very pungent, smoky suits, and was probably the thing that most interested JJ. We explored their dive boat and listened to all the sounds of the big ladder truck. She was curious, but calm the entire time. They all enjoyed her visit and told us to come back anytime.

• • •

One of the items we needed to purchase before the workshop was a set of booties for our dogs. There are several versions on the market and I wasn't sure which size or bootie would be best, so I ordered three different kinds. I suspect many of us tried the booties on our dogs prior to the workshop. I did this to make sure they would fit properly, but again the overachiever came out in me—I wanted to make sure she passed the certification and thought we needed to "study" this as well. Besides, you have to admit any video of a dog first introduced to boots is pretty darned funny. They turn into high stepping, slow-motion show ponies.

Much to JJ's dismay, I did settle on one pair of boots that fit her very well. We practiced a few times with them and she got used to wearing them. In hindsight, the funny thing about this was that the point of the exercise at the workshop was completely different than all the practicing we did before arriving to the workshop. The instructions to us were to, "bring a pair of booties" with us, not "practice with booties." Ah, the simple details. At least I wasn't the only one who had put their dog through "boot camp" practice. I will also say that those boots have been used many times in the years since the workshop for the protection of her feet. One of my co-workers noticed how rugged her boots were and commented: "JJ, you have doggie Keens!"

Taking my shoes four wheeling. For those who didn't hear why I am wearing them, we are hoping to pass our Animal-Assisted Crisis Response certification next month. For example, several teams were called in by the Red Cross in Prescott, Arizona two weeks ago to provide support following the tragic deaths of nineteen firefighters. It is very hot there, so the dogs had to wear their booties to protect their pads from burning on the asphalt as they walked to different locations.

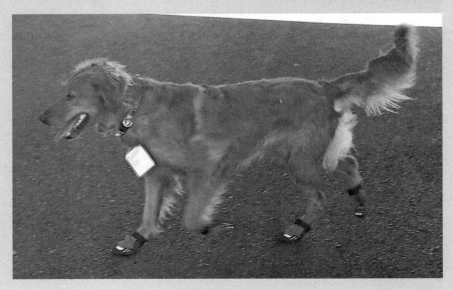

The road trip to Montana was the first long trip JJ and I had ever taken by ourselves. She was used to traveling longer distances with a large group of dogs and my husband. For one leg of the trip, I also had one of our female Labs who needed surgery with a specialist in Sun Valley, Idaho. It made the most sense for me to add a little extra time onto our trip to the workshop, drop Liz off at the vet clinic, and then pick her back up on our way back home. I had never stayed in a motel with either dog and did not anticipate their reactions. The first night, JJ was quite concerned about all the different noises she heard. We were right by the noisy door that led to our hallway and it didn't help that people were coming and going at all hours. JJ would start with her low throaty, growly warnings and on occasion it became a full on "Danger, Will Robinson" bark, which would then get Liz going. I'm not a fan of sleeping in the car and really didn't want to get kicked out of the hotel because of barking dogs, so I had JJ come up onto the bed with me so I could reach out and reassure her when she was concerned. This helped a bit, but it was a long night. To this day, when we travel for callouts, I take a "JJ" sheet with me to cover the bed and she sleeps next to me. I like to leave the place like I found it and not have dog hair all over the bed.

After dropping off Liz in Sun Valley, we arrived in Bozeman the night before the workshop. Thankfully, it was still light enough to scope out a safe area I could let JJ out to air and stretch her legs. I am from western Montana and the cool summer evenings stay light for a very long time. Even though it was a long day of driving, I was happy to get back to my home state. We were out walking in a big field, which just happened to be near a local coffee shop. In my opinion, these were the two most important finds for us during this long weekend. JJ was having a blast running around and following her nose. She came back to me with a big stick in tow, so typical of our Goldens. Her father Dash would carry about large logs and even small fallen trees. As JJ got closer, it was evident this was not your typical stick. No, this one was constructed of petrified hoof, bone, and hide. Lovely. She was proud of her elk leg treasure and sorely disappointed when I gave her the "leave it" command. She did find her prize each time we went to "her" field. Ever the optimist, she would try to find a way to stash it in the car when I wasn't looking.

We started early the next morning and knew we were all in for some long, action-packed days ahead, with enough information taken in to make our heads spin. Our workshop had a total of three team leaders and eighteen canine teams, who traveled in from Colorado, Oregon, Washington, and Montana. We were situated in a large room, but by the time we were all settled, it was very full, with dogs sprawled everywhere. All handlers were very careful to give each other space and not let the dogs get nose to nose. We had a diverse group of dogs in our group. They included Casey (Dalmatian), Roxy (Labradoodle), Hondo (Border Collie), Yuki (Samoyed), Sumi (Akita), Lucy (Cardigan Corgi), Lily (Siberian Husky), Ursa (Lab mix), Quigley (Aussie mix), and Chervil (Golden Doodle), along with a multitude of Golden Retrievers: Ben, Sierra, Zeke, Copper, Daniel, and Quinn. Over the weekend, we went through very specialized training in crisis intervention skills, also known as emotional first aid, animal behavior and stress management, critical incident stress management, incident command system training, first aid and CPR, pet first aid, and guidelines and ethics of using dogs in crisis work. All the things we learned are a part of the national standards for Animal-Assisted Crisis Response, something HOPE helped develop.

One of the key lessons in crisis response work is to remain flexible. Just like the weather in Montana, if you wait five or ten minutes during a crisis response deployment, something will change. The callouts often end up changing over time. Our presenter reminded us of this lesson throughout the workshop by pulling out a Gumby, a cue that we all needed, especially if we were getting stuck in our learning. I decided right then that a Gumby needed to come to the Hospice House, as hospice work can be like crisis response work. To this day, Gumby hangs out in different locations of the nurses' station and some of us have been known to wave him in another person's direction as a gentle reminder to relax and roll with whatever is happening at that time.

Crisis response teams need to desensitize their dogs to the common sights, sounds, and smells that might be encountered at a crisis scene, and the certification workshop had many exercises to help us with this. On the first day, we all had the opportunity to participate in some role-playing, which allowed us all not only to practice but also receive guidance and helpful feedback from experienced handlers. We also finally got to participate in the bootie dance! I was thinking, "We've got this. We have had more than enough practice." As a group, we took time to get our dogs used to wearing one or more booties. This is an exercise worthy of being taped, by the way. Looking around the room, many of the dogs were holding their first bootie-covered paw in the air with sad faces as if to tell us, "Nope. Can't. Foot is broken. Can't you people see?" By the end, most had all feet encased and had transitioned from very entertaining hippity hoppity steps to walking around with confidence. Well, most were doing this, but not all. It was very helpful to have a food-motivated dog for this exercise. JJ is perpetually starving and will do pretty much anything for a high-value treat. While we had practiced at home and at work, I hadn't counted on the stress of the workshop making this familiar task a bit more challenging. At the end of the bootie dance, we learned the purpose was for the handlers not to get all four boots on, but to find a way to help our dogs cope with being asked to do something that was new or stressful to them. The light bulb went on: I realized that while JJ may act a certain way in a familiar environment, I needed to more closely monitor her reactions to things in new settings. It was a good lesson to learn.

We had several field trips over the weekend that were very exciting not only for the dogs but for the handlers as well. The first was a trip to a fire station, where the dogs were given a chance to explore the fire trucks, turn-out gear, and even watch a ladder get extended from the truck and listen to the siren go off. We were all prepared to find a way to advocate for our dogs and help them through anything that concerned them. For many, the siren did cause the dogs to react, but walking away from it and distracting with treats was one way of coping with this. As Casey the firedog pointed out, "This was the BEST part!! You Goldens might be good at chilling in the classroom, but I know my way around a fire station!!" Casey got bored easily in the classroom when he had to hang out like a bump on a log while people talked on and on around him, but he rocked the fire station visit.

The field trips the next day were even more adventurous and put our handling skills to the test. After spending much of the morning and part of the afternoon in class, we all loaded a school bus to head to the airport. When HOPE teams are deployed on a callout or event, they are considered a working team, like a Search and Rescue team, and some airlines allow us to fly to get to the crisis response location. Unlike service dogs, HOPE AACR dogs have no legal right to be on the plane, so it is very much appreciated when they say yes. It is made clear that the dogs are not service dogs when reservations are made. Because teams may end up flying, the airport exercise helps dogs and handlers get an idea of what to expect when traveling and how to negotiate the steps necessary to get onto a flight. As we walked through the airport toward the TSA security check point, my treat bag was full of high-value training treats including cheese and liver bits. We had to climb the stairs next to an escalator to get to the screening area. Mind you, I would never get on an escalator with a dog, but I didn't think much of being on the staircase next to it. Apparently, the stairs had sent out a very scary telepathic message to JJ indicating great harm, because I had to go through almost all my treats just to keep her four feet on the ground next to me—I did not see that coming. By the time we got in line for the security check, we were almost the last dog in line, just ahead of Hondo the Border Collie. Because we would never take our collars and leashes off our dogs at any time when out in public, they remained in place and set off the metal detector. All the dogs had to have the scanning wand waved over them. It is safe to say this is not a dog's idea of a good time and here I was with only a couple of treats left in my bag. The ideal situation would be to ask the screener to let the dog sniff the wand first and have plenty of treats to distract. JJ was the seventeenth dog through, and while the TSA screener was a good sport, he was getting tired of this. Before either of us was ready, he quickly swooped the wand down over JJ and she nearly jumped out of her skin. Bad handler. I borrowed some treats from someone and she recovered just fine, but it was a good lesson. Load up with more treats than you think you would ever need when facing something like this. When I looked behind me, Hondo seemed to breeze through his screening without any fuss, which is a reminder—each dog will react to stress in a different way and what bothers one dog may not affect another. It is not always predictable, so be prepared at all times.

We loaded back into the school bus to make the trek to dinner at a local restaurant. There was plenty of room on the bus and we made sure there was only one dog per seat as a safety measure. The past two days had been quite stressful with so much sensory overload for our dogs. When dogs get stressed, they are like people and can get cranky and reactive. To make sure we didn't get too close to one another, the dogs were put on window seat while their handlers sat next to the aisle. I was focused on getting JJ in the correct spot and didn't give much thought to the setup until we were slowly driving through the streets of downtown Bozeman, stopping at several lights. I wish we had had a video camera recording of the people on the sidewalks doing double takes and pointing at the bus. All they could see was a school bus full of dogs, patiently sitting in their seats and looking out at the people. They couldn't really see the handlers because of the reflection of the evening sun. The confused looks on their faces were simply priceless. I can only imagine what I would have thought had I been in their shoes.

We were dropped off at the restaurant and escorted to a section reserved for us. When HOPE dogs are deployed, they are considered working teams during their deployment. As handlers, we do not leave our dogs in a car if the temperatures are not safe, and we can ask a restaurant if they will let us bring our dogs in, but we are honest that they are not service dogs. Service dogs have federal protection that allows them anywhere, while dogs in a therapy or crisis response role do not. Still, it is common for working crisis response teams to be invited into restaurants while deployed, especially when it is known how the teams are helping in the community. Because of this, it is important to do some onsite training.

Starky's Authentic Americana, a nice restaurant in Bozeman, has worked with teams during past certification workshops. As a group, we had to decide where people would sit and which dogs might be best suited to be near one another. Just as would happen during a callout, we had to work together to make sure we took care of business in the safest possible manner. JJ is small for a Golden, and it was easy to tuck her under a booth table with another small dog from the Pacific Northwest. Our wait staff was wonderfully patient and did a remarkable job of managing to take all our orders and delivered plates of food while making sure not to step on any tails sticking out in the aisle. The dogs were quiet and did not make a fuss, which showed on the patrons' surprised faces when it was time for all of us to leave. Imagine seeing eighteen well-mannered dogs walking out of a restaurant when you had no idea they were even in there. It was a sign of a job well done by all.

I think it was safe to say by the last morning we were all exhausted from the previous two days. I loaded up with caffeine, while JJ said goodbye to her elk leg for the last time and we headed to our last workshop day. We worked through a big disaster scenario and then it was graduation time. All teams except for one passed their certification and we had a great celebration for all the hard work everyone did, including those who helped to put on the workshop. Afterward, it was time for JJ and me to say goodbye to our new friends and make our way back to Oregon.

When we had dropped off Liz for her surgery, there were numerous reports of wildfires in the western states, including Idaho. On our first trip into Sun Valley, it was easy to see fires on the distant hills as it was dark so early in the morning. My husband teases me about being a weather and firewatcher, but I grew up with parents who did this for good reason. We were raised in western Montana in a house surrounded by trees, and forest fires started by lightning are common in the western states and can get out of control quickly. Most summers my parents would pack a fireproof box filled with important documents and sentimental items that could not be replaced. Luckily, it was never needed.

Knowing there were fires getting close to Sun Valley several days before, I had been keeping track online. Several communities were under evacuation orders by the time I left Montana, though they were still a distance from Sun Valley. By the time we picked Liz up, the valley was coated in smoke, it was hard to breathe, and there were firefighters everywhere. We drove right past the base camp for those fighting the fires, one of the situations we had talked about for possible HOPE team deployments. Several highways and roads had been closed by this point, and the whole situation was reminding me of a time a few years before JJ was born when I had been caught on the interstate in a traffic jam because of a roadside fire. I happened to have JJ's mother Gamine with me in the car at the time and traffic was barely moving, when suddenly several trees next to us lit up like a Roman candle and we had to inch our way through flames and smoke. It was a scary adrenaline rush that I would never want to repeat. After we picked up Liz, I checked to make sure our road home was clear, said a quick prayer for the firefighters, and hit the road. The smoke seemed to follow us for many miles and when we came to a bend in the road, there was fire on both sides. Oh. Joy. The entire countryside was either burning or blackened for several miles. I was jealous of the two snoring dogs in the back, their minds at ease while I white-knuckled our way past the flames. It's safe to say you'll never find me thinking firefighting would be a nice second career. When we'd made it through, I was never so happy to get back to the interstate.

Once we were home, I started going to any new location I could think of to expose JJ to different things. I had found a suspension bridge over water for pedestrians just outside a park I often stopped at when traveling back and forth to Montana. The planks sway when you walk and you can see below down to the water. I had a pocketful of treats and had JJ practice her sit-stays and down-stays all along the bridge. She handled it quite well and a few cyclists came along, commenting "What a well-trained dog." Well, yes, but the power of the treats in my hand had a lot to do with it! When we had to travel back to Montana again a few months after the workshop, I found all sorts of different places to do some impromptu training.

Oh, and You Know Who came up with the BRILLIANT idea for some training and desensitization while we were out playing. At our HOPE workshop, someone was talking about having to get the dogs on a boat, but some dogs never made it past the scary dock! So, we practiced on a very unstable dock with waves crashing into it. She didn't have bacon, so the usual treats had to do. Sheesh! I did OK, but it was a weird sensation. I have come to the conclusion that BossyPants is a bit nuts.

Our first callout happened only by chance. I had been asked by a leadership class at the local high school to give a presentation about HOPE. When I arrived at the high school, something seemed off, but I wasn't sure what it was. When I gave the presentation, the kids alternated between being very subdued and very emotional. They all did enjoy getting some time with JJ and many were excited to learn of her "hug" command. When you are a sad or stressed teenager, hugs from a dog can be a very good thing. Many of the students lined up to get a hug from JJ while having their friends get a photo of it on their phones. After my presentation, I was asked by two of the students and the teacher if I could stay to give some support. A student had recently died and her memorial service was going to be held at the school that afternoon. Since HOPE teams never self-deploy, I told them they would have to get permission from the school principal while I sent a message to my regional director to ask about the situation. Normally, HOPE would be requested ahead of time, but given the situation was immediate, we decided in this case since I was acting as a HOPE representative, we could stay if we were asked. The principal agreed and we spent some time in the guidance counselor's office and then walked around with the leadership teacher, providing support where needed. I was asked to be in the room where family members and her teammates would be gathered waiting before the memorial service began. We were quietly present, available for anyone who needed a little time with JJ. I took her lead for who might need a snuggle, including the student's parents and sister. We stayed out of the way during the memorial service but had many people stop to give JJ a quick hug.

At this point, we had nine active teams with a couple of team leaders in the Pacific Northwest. Ours had traditionally been a quiet region when it came to crises and disasters. Teams in the past had participated in scheduled events such as Operation Purple, a summer camp for military kids, but for the most part, we did not have many reasons to be called for a crisis. This changed on March 22, 2014, when a very large section of a hillside came crashing down onto a tiny community in Oso, Washington. It was a catastrophic slide that crushed everything in its path—including houses—and the debris field crossed a river and highway in a matter of minutes. I was working that day and received a message from our HOPE AACR regional director, asking teams to be on standby and let her know of our availability, just in case teams would be called out. My hospice patients had all been taken care of and it was quiet at the time, so I pulled up the local news to see what had happened. I kept thinking, "I know that town. Why do I know that town?" Many years ago, when I was a home hospice nurse in Washington State, I often would cover for the nurse who visited patients in the far northern areas of our hospice territory, so I had driven past Oso several times on the same highway now covered with up to twenty feet of mud and debris. By Sunday, the call had come for a couple of teams to deploy to the Emergency Operations Center for Snohomish County. I had some days off and was available to head north, so JJ and I were one of the first teams able to respond. At the time, the HOPE dogs had only been invited to the EOC to provide comfort to those trying their very best to cope with such a huge disaster. We continued to have people reach out to be able to do more, but it is so very important that teams never self-deploy. While well intentioned, having people show up with their therapy dogs or pets adds chaos to an already chaotic situation, especially when they have not had the training to cope with such a situation. This was happening, but we made sure those in charge knew our HOPE teams would never show up to an area uninvited.

While many people have participated in disaster drills through their work and may even have a personal emergency plan in place, I was simply dumbfounded by the enormity of what had happened and the response needed to figure out where to even start. I'm not sure anyone could dream up this scenario to prepare for it. I was careful to make sure JJ did not interfere with anyone doing their work, while at the same time watching for people who indicated they needed a minute with her. As we moved along the periphery of the EOC, watching so many different people working on their assigned tasks, people would indicate their need to spend some time with JJ. Even if it was just for thirty or sixty seconds, petting her and receiving a hug seemed to help keep them going. Many had been working for 48 hours with minimal rest in an incredibly stressful environment.

The call center manned by volunteers was also in the same building as the EOC. It was impressive to see so many offer to help, though I could quickly tell this was a very stressful assignment. A hotline had been set up for people to report those missing or found. I could only imagine how frantic people were about loved ones they were not able to reach. JJ spent time alternating between the EOC and the call center, giving out as much comfort as she could. By the end of that day, the numbers had jumped to an incredible 176 persons possibly missing. The sadness and defeat showed on everyone's faces. While this number would probably decrease as people were able to check in, it was a staggering way to end the day as the Public Information Officer released this number of presumed missing to the press.

On the first day, I met someone at the EOC who worked at the 911 dispatch center that had taken the emergency calls at the time of the slide just two days earlier. He took a brochure from me and spoke to his supervisor about us, then by the end of the day, HOPE teams, including JJ and me, were called to respond. The next day we headed to the dispatch center after a short morning shift at the EOC. JJ did her magic with everyone and was very well received. As one person reflected, "JJ climbed into my lap and helped with a bad call. The woman's best friend had just been recovered and she wanted confirmation. She was upset with me and venting, frustrated, and grieving." It was hard, but when we left, we knew we'd done good work and that some incredible teams would be taking over.

People at the Emergency Operations Center were happy to see me back this morning. "The hugging dog is back!" So, I had to pass out some hugs. The Puparazzi was out in force, including a FEMA photographer with a REALLY big camera.

I knew as time went on that teams would likely be invited to other areas to provide comfort. With only nine teams in our region, we were very limited in how many people could respond. As JJ and I drove home, the call was going out to other regions to determine if anyone was available. Our dogs' welfare comes first, so when we deploy, we work in shifts of typically three to four hours long and the teams are only deployed for a few days at a time. Because of the hospice work JJ does, I make sure to limit our deployments to only one or two days at a time. HOPE AACR teams are volunteers, so those of us who travel to areas outside of our local region often absorb the cost. At times, there is grant money available to help defray some of the costs, but not always.

We did make one more trip to Oso three weeks later to provide support. By this time, HOPE teams were staged all over giving comfort to a variety of people in different settings. Teams from Colorado, California, and Montana had taken turns helping us out. On our second deployment, we got to meet two of the teams from the Pacific Southwest region.

By the time I had returned to the hotel that evening, JJ and I were both exhausted although she had the luxury of power napping on the road. I didn't have the energy to even try to find a restaurant where I could take her for dinner, and eating in bed seemed like a lovely idea, so we walked from the hotel across the street to an Irish Pub to order take-out. JJ and I were still in our HOPE uniforms as we waited in the restaurant lobby for my food when some people walked by us as they were leaving, and one asked what kind of dog JJ was. Two of them were first responders in the area and were aware how the HOPE dogs had been helping. They were with a woman who had just lost a close loved one and she spent some time petting and talking to JJ before they moved on. It reminded me how these special connections can happen at any time.

On our last day, we were asked to go to Darrington, a community that had essentially been cut off from the rest of the county when the slide hit. One route to the west side remained, but it was a remote highway that took at least three times as long to drive, so Seattle City Light made their utility access road available—a makeshift route directly to Darrington—but it was a one-way route with a pilot car that took quite a while to navigate.

The drive toward Darrington was still familiar to me from so many years ago as a hospice nurse. The contrast of those who had lost their lives so unexpectedly and my day-to-day work in the area making sure those at the end of their lives died peacefully, weighed heavily on my mind. As I drove along, I naturally began to reminisce about the last time I made this trip as a nurse. It was Christmas Eve and we had had a winter storm, which brought quite a bit of snow to the area. In the Puget Sound, almost everything closes when there is snow or ice. The utility crews have few snowplows and are not equipped to keep many of the roads open. Since I had an all-wheel drive vehicle, I was asked to take my social worker partner with me to admit a new hospice patient who couldn't wait until after Christmas. Because of the snow, the drive took at least twice as long as it normally did, but it was a beautiful winter wonderland and, since I was a Montana girl, I absolutely loved it. When we got to the house, I led the way because I had on snow boots and Karen didn't, so I made sure to shorten my steps through the knee-high snow creating a path for her. We briefly talked with the elderly wife, who was alone in caring for her husband. We only needed one glance at him in the recliner to know time was very short for him. As was typical for us, Karen guided the wife to the kitchen to sign papers and talk with her while I attended to her husband. They reminded me of my own Montana kin, the generations that led to my sister and me—strong, independent, proud, and determined people. The kind that takes care of one another, but does not ask for help. We had brought an emergency supply of comfort meds, knowing pharmacy hours would be limited at Christmas. He looked uncomfortable in the chair and, after asking his wife if I could get him to bed, I got to business taking care of him. He had end stage cancer, though I don't remember what kind. I do remember he was tiny and light as a feather as I knelt and picked him up to carry him to their bed. He was barely responsive, but tucked his head next to my cheek in relief. I got him cleaned up and settled, giving a small amount of pain medication for his obvious discomfort, then I showed his wife how to provide the care and medications he needed. We left supplies for her, knowing he most likely would not make it through the night, and made sure she had the twenty-four-hour phone number to reach our on-call nurse at any time. These tender, intimate moments of providing care to someone who is dying is the essence of hospice nursing and what keeps me doing this work so many years later.

By the time I made it to the access road, those memories caused tears to stream down my face, and I did my best to pull myself together before I had to show my pass. This was the first day people could use this road to drive through, and even though I had been told what to expect, driving past the edge of the rubble pile and seeing the slide area was simply unbelievable and hard to even process. I had heard the same sentiments from people in the EOC who had been out here, but until you saw it in person, there was just no way to imagine the devastation. Once I made it to Darrington, I found a place to let JJ out and we went for a walk to decompress before we started doing any visits. The great thing about having a dog partner like JJ is her willingness to participate in playtime. JJ was more than willing to chase a ball and do her version of "fetch," which involves her chasing after a ball, toy, or bumper, picking it up, running a few steps away from me and then dropping the object and then rolling on it. It cracks me up every time and was just what I needed at that moment. We spent time with the Red Cross workers who were helping support community members, as well as with workers in the FEMA tent.

By the time we went back over the access road to head home, JJ and I both were exhausted. I could only give a silent note of thanks and prayers of strength for those helping as I drove back by the pile, knowing so many people and dogs were out there still searching. It took four months to locate the remains of the last of forty-three people who perished.

• • •

On the first-year anniversary of the slide, HOPE teams were again asked to be present to offer comfort. We first went back to the 911 dispatch center to visit those we had seen one year before. In the time since, there had been more traumatic calls these dispatchers had to deal with, including the Marysville High School shooting. JJ passed out her hugs to everyone, making sure they all had a chance to rub her belly as well. The next day, we were assigned to one of the family buses as they were shuttled to the slide site for a memorial ceremony near the forty-three trees planted in honor of the victims. It was a raw and emotional first-year anniversary, but a necessary commemoration. Our dogs spent a lot of time giving their love.

In between callouts, I tried to find opportunities to do different kinds of training with JJ. Just as HOPE members must have continuing education each year for renewal, I figured JJ should be doing her own version of it. When we were in Seattle on our last callout, I realized I had forgotten another item to introduce her to—there always seems to be something I have missed.

When we were in Seattle over the weekend, I had to go out in my rain-coat and BossyPants just had to take this evil thing called an umbrella. Like a typical Pacific Northwest person, she has one, but never uses it. Which means I jumped out of my skin when she popped that puppy open. YIKES! So, we spent this morning working on it with a HUGE umbrella used for the puppies for their swimming pool.

Before the Oso slide happened, I had been reaching out to my local community and had set up a time to talk about HOPE with one of the local school district's Crisis Response Coordinators. Shortly after we had returned from our first trip to Oso, I received a call from her asking if we could do a "working interview." A young boy had died and the Crisis Response Team was going to be at his school to help support the staff and teachers as they shared the news with the kids. We weren't sure how many dog teams would be needed, but at the time we only had three active teams in Oregon. I arrived at the school and had Amy and Casey, JJ's Dalmatian friend, on standby, not sure of what the need would be. We started in this boy's classroom while teachers prepared to give the news. Shortly afterward, we decided it would be a good idea to have another dog to help and Casey was called in. The kids absolutely loved the dogs. Since JJ and Casey were friends, we needed to keep them separate when we were in the same room, otherwise, they would want to play together. When on callouts, the HOPE dogs wear their uniform, a green vest. The vests have pockets on them, and this is where I keep JJ's calling cards to hand out to people. The kids learned very quickly where these cards were kept and we handed them all out by mid-day. Many of the kids drew pictures for the dogs, some had serious conversations with them, and some simply wanted a quick pet before moving on. When we debriefed, one of the Crisis Team members said to me: "I don't know how you got here, but it was pure genius!" At this school, the teachers, staff, and students hand out "gecko cards" to those who have been respectful and responsible with others. At the end of the day, a student came up and gave JJ one. To this day, the gecko card is in one of her vest pockets and has gone on every callout.

The kids decided we made a good boyfriend and girlfriend and should have puppies. When The Bossy One asked what the puppies would look like, they said "white with golden spots!" When we went on another callout with the same crisis team several months later, they told me the kids still talk about us.

After this first callout, it became standard for HOPE teams to be a part of the Crisis Response team when needed. Unfortunately, we have had several deaths that have impacted the schools, especially at one high school, which has had to deal with a lot of loss over the past two years. In Oregon, we are slowly getting more teams certified, but often people are not available right away. I am fortunate to have a fair amount of flexibility with my schedule, so JJ often participates.

We continue to reach out to the local school districts to make sure they are aware of this volunteer service available to them. While we are accessible for out of area callouts, serving our local community remains a passion for me. Knowing how much good has come from having HOPE dogs help in our local schools brings great satisfaction. The Crisis Team Coordinator for the school district, the person who leads the central command post in the event of a crisis, had this to say after we met:

> "Unfortunately, we have had many deaths in our district of students, staff, coaches, parents, and twice now we have had to respond to multiple deaths on one day. As the coordinator, my job is incredibly stressful and I have to be able to command several responses, twenty to fifty response team members, several schools, communication with the staff, students, parents, and school district, and just make sure we respond in an organized and responsive manner. At any point during the day, I can be dealing with students and staff affected by the death, law enforcement, the family of the deceased, et cetera and many times all come at once. When JJ and Tracy arrive, I request a minute or two with JJ. That brief minute when she gives me a hug grounds me and gives me a quick minute of solace. I am immediately ready to jump back into the rigorous and incredibly intense situation. Twice now I have witnessed JJ finding the most impacted person in a group of people to snuggle up to. It still brings tears to my eyes when thinking about a memorial service for one of our students that was held at one of our high schools. This student had died very unexpectedly and of an unknown medical condition. There were hundreds of students, staff, and family in the auditorium and Tracy and JJ sat on the floor near the choir who had been deeply impacted by this death. JJ inched herself around the kids and moved to the floor next to the father of the child who had died. JJ lay at his feet during most of the service. It was an incredibly spiritual moment!"

As I said, there is one high school that has been affected by so much loss in a short time. As their principal reflected, "JJ is awesome! As soon as she steps on the scene, a calming and soothing sense pervades the environment. I've watched JJ assist so many in times of tragedy and crisis and I am one of those fortunate people. For me, the power of animals to comfort us during distress is unparalleled by any drug or meditation."

Not even three months after the Oso landslide, another tragedy struck the Puget Sound. This time it was a shooting on the campus of Seattle Pacific University—one student was killed and two others wounded. One of the big challenges for teams was the number of pet dogs on campus. After the shooting, one of the local radio stations put out a call for people to bring their dogs to the campus, which while well intentioned, was not helpful. We had response teams at SPU when these pet dogs descended on the campus and let's just say it is extremely challenging to try to do crisis work with a lot of untrained or undertrained dogs and handlers. There was so much effort by the handlers to make sure they could keep their dogs safe and away from other animals that for a while, it got in the way of us doing the job we were supposed to be doing. Volunteering as a HOPE AACR team requires a lot of training before teams are ever prepared to go on scene somewhere.

On occasion, I have kept in contact with some of those we have met at HOPE callouts, and I cherish the messages they send to me.

"I graduated from Seattle Pacific University, then went to work there for ten years before moving on to work at a nearby church. The day after the shooting, I went to SPU with several of my colleagues to meet and comfort the many students, staff, and faculty that attended our church. That is how I met JJ. After meeting with several students and while waiting to meet up with another, I walked across campus to stand across the street from the building where the shooting occurred. When I had been a student, it had housed all the sciences. Since I was studying biology, I spent quite a bit of time there. After I graduated, I took a job as an office assistant in that same building. I knew the people who worked there. I had walked through those lobby doors more times than I could count. I had hired student-building monitors to sit at the entrance desk where the young man who stopped the shootings had been sitting. It was heavy and hard to see this place that had been such an important part of my life indelibly marked by gunfire and death. My community had been violated. I stood with one of my former professors and wept and prayed. Soon after that, I headed toward the large green space on campus known as the loop to meet up with a student leader. While I was waiting for her, I noticed JJ and her handler. I watched as JJ stood calmly as a student just petted her over and over again. The student didn't say much, but you could see on her face what comfort JJ brought.

After the student left, I walked over to meet JJ. I was tired and heartsick, but I was there to comfort those directly impacted by the shooting, not to seek my own solace. I just greeted and petted JJ and briefly talked to her handler, Tracy. I was surprised, as I then walked to my next student meeting, how much calmer I felt. Just those few moments of peace and acceptance, without having to explain anything to JJ (or Tracy), gave me a moment of rest and encouragement that carried me through the rest of the afternoon as I held weeping students, listened to their stories and questions and attended a prayer service for the campus. JJ and I only interacted for maybe five minutes, but I think that day would have been much tougher for me and so many others if she and her fellow crisis dogs had not been there."

A few months after SPU, another shooting happened at a high school in Marysville, Washington. Because we were in the middle of some very intense weeks at our Hospice House, I chose not to deploy with JJ. It's not always the right time or situation, and it is important as a handler to recognize this and know my limitations. By this time, our region had grown by many teams so there were others who could deploy to help the students, staff, and community cope.

I decided the following year to take JJ on a great adventure and go to our HOPE annual conference, which was held in Charleston, South Carolina that year. It would mean traveling by plane, a first for JJ and for me as a handler. In addition to meetings, there would be activities and plenty of those "training opportunities" JJ loves so much. On the day before we flew out, we all heard the heartbreaking news of the shooting deaths of several members of the AME church in Charleston. I had many people asking if we would have teams responding, but at this point, it was too early to know if anyone would be asked to deploy. We would have plenty of teams to choose from, and it certainly was on the minds of everyone as we traveled.

We had been visiting Montana, so flew our first leg on what my parents always affectionately called a "puddle jumper." I learned a small airport meant it didn't take long to get through security, even with a dog. Once on the plane, she curled up and was happy to sleep on the short journey. I was happy that JJ is a petite Golden as it gave me a bit more legroom.

When we reached Seattle, I took her to the indoor "airing" location that had fake grass and a fire hydrant. JJ looked at me as if I had completely lost my mind by asking her to go to the bathroom indoors and she was having none of it. Luckily, we had a long layover and had the time to go outside to a "real" bathroom area and still have time to make it back through security. She handled the scanning wand like a champ, but I was also ready with plenty of treats.

On our second leg of the flight, we were seated next to a very well-known aviation consultant and former airline pilot from Seattle. I had lived in Seattle for a long time and quickly recognized him, as I had seen him appear on national television many times when he was consulted during major aviation disasters. I didn't want to bother him during the flight, so just said a quick hello and asked if he would be OK with JJ sitting on the floor next to him, which is what I have always asked people we are flying next to.

As we approached our destination, it was evident we were flying directly into a storm. I've never experienced such turbulence and could see lightning strikes outside the window. Flying has never bothered me, but by this point, the plane was bouncing around severely and I was getting nervous. My seatmate was starting to take notice of the storm as well, but in the casual way I might approach a medical emergency as a nurse when trying not to alarm anyone. I couldn't resist and said, "So, I hate to bother you, but this seems like some fairly severe weather we are in." He talked about the general way pilots try to fly around storms and some technical things about radar that went over my head. I finally asked if there was anything to be concerned about and he told me, "Only if you see me put on a parachute." I was happy when we landed and amazed that JJ slept through the entire ordeal. It was a relief when we finally got to our hotel in Charleston.

It was clear when we landed that many of our planned outdoor activities for the conference were going to be put on hold because of an incredible heat wave. We did venture out in the mornings, but the heat indices by midday were between 110 to 114 degrees, and it didn't cool off much at night. We spent much of our time inside in the air conditioning, as neither JJ nor I were prepared to cope with the weather conditions and did not have time to acclimate. Those of us in the Pacific Northwest think it's hot when it's eighty degrees with minimal humidity. Our HOPE teams were invited to a prayer vigil, but since the top priority in crisis response is the safety of the dogs, I knew we wouldn't attempt to be a part of it. For most of our dogs, it was far too hot and humid to safely deploy once we were asked. As much as everyone wanted to be as supportive of the community as possible, the situations aren't always appropriate for all dog teams to be deployed.

One of the scheduled events was dinner at a local restaurant with all the HOPE members and dogs. The dogs have all been trained to relax under or right next to a table while food is being served. We filled the upstairs area and not one dog made a peep. JJ was happy to get out of the heat and settle in for a nap. We had many compliments from those at the restaurant. People could not believe how well behaved such a large group of dogs was; a sentiment shared everywhere we went in Charleston. On the shuttle back to the hotel, we slowly inched our way through the throngs of people walking to the prayer vigil for the nine people killed at the church. We did have some southern teams including a Labradoodle named George and Porsha, a Saint Bernard, who were at the vigil that night giving support, and several teams stayed after the conference to continue giving comfort. I could have easily changed flights to another day, but JJ and I were melting in the southern humidity. I knew we were not the right team for the job.

While we were in the airport waiting for the plane to start our journey home, several people were very happy to hear they could pet JJ. I had heard of many airports using therapy dogs to help decrease the stress for travelers and it was evident how helpful this could be just in the thirty minutes of seeing people interact with her. Because she was wearing her HOPE vest, many people assumed she was a service dog. Once people saw they could pet JJ, we had a line with people wanting to spend time with her. As she always does, she took it in stride, giving out love until it was our turn to board our plane. For the record, you can fit a human and a JJ-sized dog in an airplane lavatory. As a HOPE canine handler, I cannot leave my dog unattended or with someone who is not a member of HOPE, so when I had to go to the bathroom, JJ had to join me. It required some contortion-ist-like maneuvering, but we got it done and the look of surprise on the faces of my fellow travelers was priceless.

Trains, planes, and automobiles (or airport shuttles). We aren't quite done with the adventure yet. You can probably imagine how much I have been exposed to this trip. It is an example of our ongoing training and desensitization to new things, so we can focus on the task at hand when on a callout.

In the words of one of our fellow HOPE members, "This is what these dogs do. They help people to forget, even for a moment, and to breathe, and even to laugh." It has been an honor to get to volunteer this way with JJ. I can only hope to have dogs like her in the future to partner with once the time comes for JJ to retire.

13

One of the most common comments said to those of us who do hospice work is, "That must be so depressing." Actually, it isn't depressing, although all of us have had times when it can get overwhelming. For those of us who have done end-of-life work for a long time, it simply is *a good fit*. Death is a normal part of the life cycle, even if so many people want to pretend they can avoid it. We can be caring, compassionate, and present during a very sad part of peoples' lives, yet most of us know we must maintain some boundaries and separation if we are to be successful long term in guiding others through this journey. And when it comes to our own people, we grieve and cope just like anyone else.

The longer those of us do hospice work, the more prepared most of us are when it comes to our own loved ones dying. One of the nurses I worked with when I first started hospice said it best when her mother died. "This is why I brought my mother home from the hospital, to die in my bedroom, surrounded by twenty-some progeny. My career trajectory is complete. I awoke in the morning to find Dad sitting quietly at her side. She had breathed her last breath probably an hour earlier. He was calm. I sat calmly beside him. We knew we did what we could, and what we should. I wish this for all of your loved ones."

Since the Hospice House opened, we have taken care of some of our own, and there is something special about helping care for each other in a way we couldn't before the Hospice House was built. It certainly is more emotional and difficult for us all, but what a gift we can give to our colleagues.

"On Mom's final day Tracy was there to ease our minds and JJ was doing her job that day as well. JJ made frequent visits to Mom's room. At one point, she just laid in the room by the door. I, of course, thought that was a sign that today was the day. A little later, she came back with her blanket and then I was certain! That night we watched her favorite show 'Wheel of Fortune' one last time together. I told her it was okay to go once it was over, but apparently, she had other plans. My girls had prom that day, but I wasn't going to leave Mom's side to join the festivities, so I showed her a picture of my daughters looking beautiful. Of course, she didn't have her eyes open to see it, but it made me feel better. Mom always loved seeing the girls all dressed up. My sister, niece, and I were all with Mom holding her hand when she passed. She died at 11:12 p.m. Saturday night, just as prom was ending. I'm certain Mom was watching over the girls one last time. And the final very touching act of kindness came from Tracy. As we were sitting with Mom waiting for the funeral home, JJ comes into Mom's room after being off duty for several hours. Of course, that was probably my biggest cry ever! It was a small Walkout, but JJ was in the lead. Thank you."

Simply put, some days are just more difficult. When it's time to care for our own people, it hits very close to home. It's time for one of our nurses' brother to say goodbye after a very brief battle with cancer, and I'm here to give her love. There was some creative problem solving to get him to the Hospice House from the hospital today, fulfilling one of his wishes.

As I have become a more seasoned hospice nurse over time, my personal experiences with loss have changed. My maternal grandfather was the first person in my family who died when I had only been a hospice nurse for a couple of years. My mother's parents, our Nana and Papa, were quite a hoot. Imagine the politest gentleman you could ever meet married to a wild Greek woman. He picked her up after her high school graduation and they headed to the church to get married at eighteen. They were quintessential Montanans: they had little money, but worked hard and took care of their family. My mom and her siblings were born in their cabin and grew up eating food gathered through fishing, hunting, and gardening. Outdoor activities, including camping, were always on the agenda. My nana was the one who taught most of her granddaughters the important things in life, including how to pee outside in the woods and avoid getting poked by any bushes. Since most of our family was involved in the ski business, Christmas Eve was our traditional family get together after the ski lifts quit running for the day and before everyone headed back to work Christmas morning. Three generations would gather at Nana and Papa's house for dinner, but the highlight for all of us young kids was waiting for Santa to arrive with presents. We would wait to hear the sleigh bells and the sounds of hooves on the roof, knowing Santa's jolly self would be coming through the door at any minute.

Papa was diagnosed with liver cancer a short time before he and my grandmother celebrated their sixtieth wedding anniversary. Milestone anniversaries were always celebrated with big parties in our family. He was thin and jaundiced, but able to participate with so many friends and family members. One month later, I received a phone call that he was in the hospital and was not doing well at all. I made it back that evening and went to visit him. He was very weak but assured me he was comfortable. When I think back to that time, it was clear I hadn't yet combined my hospice nursing knowledge with my role as a granddaughter. I can remember many of the details that evening, and if this happened today, I would have been very clear that he was actively dying. I can recognize that in a heartbeat now, especially after all of these years, but at the time, I didn't make the connection. We got the call in the early morning that he had died and like so many of my hospice family members I have cared for, I felt extremely guilty that I hadn't been there.

While my nana had had some chronic health problems, none were at the time life threatening. However, I did warn my family that after sixty years of marriage, she was going to feel lost and for them not to be surprised if she declined suddenly. In hospice work, we have seen many spouses die within a few months, especially when they were married for a long period of time. Sure enough, two months after Papa died, I got a phone call that Nana was not doing well and she was going to the hospital. She was nonresponsive but holding on. I most likely would not make it back in time, so I had the nurse hold the phone to her ear so I could say my goodbyes. As I spoke to my mom throughout the day, it sounded as though she was comfortable. In fact, no one could understand why she was lingering. We often tell our hospice families how sometimes people will hold on for important dates or events before letting go. I kept thinking it over and in the evening, it finally dawned on me. I called my mom and told her, "It's Papa's birthday tomorrow. Make sure she knows. Tell her even if she doesn't seem to be responding." Sure enough, not long after midnight on his birthday, she took her leave from her body to be with him once again.

Fast forward many years to the phone call I will never forget. "After all the tests ruling everything else out, I think your mom has Motor Neuron Disease, but we need to have her seen by a specialist." I knew this meant he was suspecting Amyotrophic Lateral Sclerosis, also known as ALS, a progressive neurodegenerative disease that is always fatal. I had been back in Montana the month before going to doctor appointments as we tried to sort out her symptoms. Her main complaint was feeling "flat footed" with subsequent falls. Most patients diagnosed with ALS present with the same kind of initial symptoms that Mom had. As the family nurse, I was always the one to help when Mom had any health concerns, although sometimes it was a challenge because she would minimize anything wrong with her. I would always shake my head at her though because she would refer to her stroke as "the time I got sick" and didn't consider herself a cancer survivor since she only needed surgery, not chemo or radiation. The Christmas right before her diagnosis, she had another big fall in the kitchen. We found out later that she fell so hard she knocked a head-sized hole in the drywall. True to her nature, she made my dad patch it up before company came over for Christmas Eve so that no one would be the wiser, and my sister and I learned of this a couple of months later. When I have hospice family members talk to me about their stubborn, independent parent who won't let them help, I can relate.

There are only a handful of clinics across the country that specialize in

ALS. Since it can be difficult to diagnose, we were encouraged to take Mom either to Washington State, Minnesota, or California. Since I had lived and worked in the Seattle area for so long, we chose to go to the Virginia Mason Medical Center in Seattle to meet with a specialist. I was used to navigating the local traffic and knew the area hospitals well. My parents flew in from Montana, my sister from Utah, and I picked them all up at the airport after driving from Oregon. Even though Mom had researched this doctor, it really didn't dawn on her what his neurological specialty was. It's no wonder considering that Motor Neuron Disease is so vague sounding, and I hadn't shared my suspicions before our visit. The whole medical team was kind and compassionate, as they put Mom through the myriad of diagnostic tests. To fully rule out any other diagnosis, she had to give more vials of blood. As we sat in the waiting room of the lab, staring at a tropical fish tank, she finally said to me "But isn't that Lou Gehrig's Disease?" and I had to answer "Yes." We went back to this hospital a second time for the final set of tests to confirm ALS, but once we had a definitive diagnosis, her pragmatism won out. She convened a family conference that same day in Seattle and gave us our marching orders. The next day, she and my dad returned to Montana to resume her care at home. Even though Mom's symptoms were progressing rapidly, the doctors felt a short time in a Whitefish-area hospital rehab might help her to maintain some strength and learn how to compensate, as she got weaker. She was a trooper and went in for a few weeks and worked very hard, enjoying the therapy dogs that would visit.

One of my trips back to Montana with Callie was arranged to coincide with my mother's transfer home. It was also at that time when the local hospice program signed her onto their service. She required a wheelchair by this time and had worked with occupational therapy to be able to do things like bake cookies, something she did frequently. I knew she was working so hard because she believed it would all be fine and normal once she got back to her own home. She fully expected to return home, ditch the wheelchair, and get on with the tasks of everyday life—after all, it had only been a few weeks earlier when she was walking, albeit falling at times, and doing many things normal for her. One of the hardest things to witness was her crestfallen face when she realized the wheelchair was there to stay, and because of this home was no longer what she envisioned. When someone has such a rapidly progressing disease, it is hard to come to terms with these unexpected changes. The collision of her worlds—past and present with an unknown future—played across her face in an emotional tidal wave in the kitchen that day. With tears in my eyes, I turned away to give her that private space she needed, while Callie did her best to comfort her. My mother was not fond of "water works" as she called those salty, drippy things that leaked from her eyes. It was especially unfortunate that she had a common condition associated with ALS by the fancy name of pseudobulbar affect, which caused sudden and involuntary crying jags, embarrassing Mom tremendously. She was always the kind to pick herself up by the bootstraps and get on with things. I only wish her voice would have been able to hold out so the hospice social worker could have taped her stories. She had some doozies over the years.

It was clear from her rapid decline, that Mom had the ultra-speedy form of ALS. We spoke with her local physicians and made it clear that we would let nature take its course; there would be no life-prolonging measures. In fact, she was a bit miffed that she couldn't come to Oregon with me to participate in Physician-Assisted Death since being a current resident of Oregon is one of the requirements, but I pointed out that her disease progression was so rapid we were looking only at a few months. Until then, we would focus on keeping her comfortable. I attended an appointment with her local neurologist, who wanted to discuss with Mom her options for prolonged care, and I don't think he was quite prepared for the frank talk I led us to. My mom and I had already sorted through these choices before speaking to her medical team and she had decided: no extreme measures. I relayed those wishes accordingly. Of course, he probably wasn't used to having a bossy hospice nurse daughter to deal with either. We can be a force of nature when required, and I was having none of his redirecting the talk to tube feeding or BiPAP (pressurized air to help keep the lungs open) when Mom had already said no to these things. While I appreciated his desire to make sure we knew of all options available to her, over the years I have seen medical providers push for decisions the patient does not necessarily want. I knew Mom had made her decision and would find a way to haunt us all if we did not abide by her wishes.

During the first week at home, she declined each day. I could pivot transfer her to a wheelchair, but there would be no way Dad could do this alone when I was gone. It's rare to have an older house set up for wheelchair access, and their house was no exception. The day came when Mom and I both fell while I was trying to transfer her, and it was clear something would have to change. We tried having hired caregivers, but that lasted all of four hours—neither of my parents was fond of having strangers in their home. So, we found a facility for her that had a private room and was nice, all things considered.

I visited every three weeks, usually making the trip with Callie as my sidekick. She was not only my personal therapy dog but was a comfort and distraction for my parents. Mom and I would go to lunch and our motto was: life is short; eat dessert first. I got to hear a lot of great stories I hadn't heard before when friends and family would visit. I wish I would have either been writing these down or recording them. I considered it a privilege to be there, no matter how sad and difficult. It was an honor to spend time with this incredible lady who raised me and to bear witness to the loving bond between my parents. I wanted to be nowhere else, and I was thankful that Tellus could arrange his schedule so I could be away so often. As I often tell my hospice patients, it is a gift to allow your adult children to help. I was blessed she allowed me the opportunity.

My parents loved their twenty-fifth anniversary celebration and since we obviously wouldn't be able to celebrate their fiftieth, I decided to see if we could do something on their anniversary. They had made it forty-five years. We got permission from the facility to have a small party. By the time we were planning the party, Mom would fatigue very quickly, but still, it pleased her to make sure I had the names of those she wanted to invite. With some close friends and family, the party was a success, although Dad would have been perfectly fine to skip the whole thing. It was exhausting for Mom, but an important last milestone to celebrate and was she happy to have her girls and sons-in-law home to share it with, along with friends and family.

Anticipatory grief is the reaction that occurs before an impending loss. In hospice, we talk about it all the time. Now it was my turn to experience it. Just as there are waves of grief that could sneak up when you least expect it, the same can be true for anticipatory grief. That year, buying anniversary cards for my parents, as well as Mother's Day cards for my mother, was terribly bittersweet; they would be the last cards I would ever give her. There are many last moments experienced that run through your mind, and it's all a normal part of the process, both before and after someone dies. It isn't easy, but knowing these things are normal can be helpful.

The call came from Mom's hospice nurse that she was declining rapidly three days after Callie's puppies had arrived. I had just finished seeing my last home hospice patient and was fueling up my car, and I had to make some frantic arrangements. While I was due to fly out a couple of days later, I felt it was imperative I get there as soon as possible. I had the feeling my mother was going to wait for me, and I didn't want her to have an even more drawn out dying process. I made a quick call to my work supervisor and then the airline company. Tellus was driving back from the Midwest and was, in fact, in Montana when I got that call. With young puppies at home, one of us needed to be there, so he confirmed he would drive fourteen hours straight so I could leave early. I threw some clothes together while Callie went outside to air. I left her with food and water, knowing she would be just fine with her puppies until Tellus got home.

I don't even remember the drive to the airport, but I had somehow made it with time to spare and was able to catch an earlier flight, which would give me a bit more time to make sure I made the connecting flight. Luckily, my sister, Kelly, was already with my parents in Whitefish. It was too hard on Dad to sit at her bedside for very long, and I remember calling my sister and telling her I was on my way, asking her to just stay with Mom until I got there. She put the phone handset up to my mother's ear so she could hear me herself. "I'm on my way," I said. "But it's going to take me a few hours. It's okay if you can't wait for me to get there. We'll all be OK. I know it's getting time for you to go." For the most part, I held it together at the airport, but then we sat on the plane at the gate for the longest time not moving. It was finally announced that they were working on a mechanical issue found during the flight check. Why, oh why, had I changed to this earlier flight? We were still sitting and waiting as I watched the plane from my original schedule taxi out to the runway. There are only a couple of flights into the small airport of Kalispell and with each ticking minute, it was clear that I would not make the connection once we made it to Seattle—that's when I lost it. I burst into sobbing, ugly tears, knowing I had told Mom I would be there in a few hours, but my journey would run into the next day. Because I knew deep down she would wait for me, and I didn't want to put her through this agony. Once we finally got into the air, I believed we would land too late, but it turned out the flight attendant, who had listened to my tearful story, had relayed it to the captain. He so kindly radioed ahead to hold the connecting plane. There were a few of us trying to make that flight, but I can say I was the most relieved when we did.

One of Mom's friends picked me up at the airport right around midnight and took me to the hospital. With my sister and me at her bedside, Mom died about three hours later. I will forever be grateful to my husband, for somehow making it back home so I could get to Mom in time; to Callie, for knowing I could leave her with her puppies with no worries while Tellus made his way home; and to Kelly, for making sure Mom had one of us with her.

When I was visiting my parents' house a couple of weeks before Mom died, Dad and I were commenting on the lack of birds at the feeders that year, even when Callie wasn't around to chase them off. After Mom died, my sister and I started working on her obituary. In the evening, I tweaked our draft a bit to add, "She helped to create a haven for the deer and birds in their back yard, taking the occasional visits by pesky bears, skunks, and turkeys in stride." Well, the next morning my sister, Dad, and I were out on the deck enjoying some coffee with the fresh air. There was a deer at the feeding block, as usual, but there was melodious chaos with birds EVERYWHERE! Kelly said it was like we were inside an aviary. They were flying by our heads, zipping about everywhere in a behavior none of us had ever seen before. It was over quickly and then they were gone, except for a few. We looked at each other and said, "Yes, ma'am, you have our attention!"

Naturally, we were concerned about Dad after Mom died. I know the one thing that kept him alive was their dog Jazz. She was an older dog, but managed to keep going despite her health problems until early 2013, two and a half years after Mom died. Once Jazz died, we had talked to Dad about bringing one of our dogs to keep him company, and he had agreed. He liked the idea of having Gamine around, so we started teaching her how to use a ramp to get in and out of a vehicle. We had her groomed and made a trip back to Whitefish with her the summer after Jazz died. We enjoyed our visit, but at the end of it, Dad told us that he didn't want to keep Gamine because he was afraid something would happen to him and it could be a couple of days before anyone would know to check on her. He was open that he was just waiting his turn to join Mom. In hospice work, most of us have known one, or many, surviving spouses who simply don't want to live without their partner of so many years. There actually is a condition called broken heart syndrome that is recognized by the medical community. My sister and I would typically check in by phone with Dad at different times during the week. He also had a friend who lived in Arizona, and they would Skype daily at 11:00 a.m. But other than grocery shopping and attending church, my dad did not have much of a social life and tended to stay at home.

Two months after we had returned from our Montana trip, I got a call from Tellus one evening while I was still at work. He had just gotten a phone call from Dad's friend, reporting that Dad had missed the last three days of Skyping and wasn't answering his phone. I was a little confused as to why Tellus got the phone call, but we found out later that Dad had given Tellus' number as his emergency contact information to everyone, including his friend in Arizona. As I called the sheriff's office in town to request a welfare check, my biggest worry was that Dad was down and couldn't move. I fully expected that if he wasn't incapacitated, Dad was gone and with Mom, but I had to answer the deputy's questions first. "No, there are no firearms in the house. Well, there is a black powder rifle hanging above the downstairs fireplace, but it's decorative." "Yes, you will be able to enter without a problem. My parents have never locked the doors. Ever."

"No, I actually expect you will find he has died. He has a cardiac history and his bride of forty-five years died three years ago."

"No, no animals in the home unless the black bear he photographed off the deck found his way into the house."

"Oh, and please leave the sliding door open. Yes, I'm sure. We need to get in without breaking down the door once we arrive."

Even though my heart was racing, we had all expected this for some time and my family has always coped with humor. Top that with my dark hospice humor, and I'm sure that this poor deputy thought he was dealing with a nutty daughter. When I got the call back after their check, I was relieved to know he had in fact died. Dad would have been livid to survive something like a stroke or a broken hip. The deputy told me they found him on the couch, with the Saturday paper on his lap, a beer by his side and the TV on, no doubt set originally to college football. They were required to do a brief investigation, but found nothing that concerned them. "He looks like he just fell asleep."

When Tellus and I got into my parents' house, the first thing I noticed was the big stack of paperwork sitting by the kitchen phone. It had not been there in July when we had visited. For the longest time, my mom was always reminding me where the important papers were kept and where the safe deposit key was, and Dad took on giving this annual reminder once Mom died. To make things simple, my sister and I have always had our names on their accounts and on the safety deposit list as well. Have I mentioned we come from practical parents? Considering this pile of paperwork he'd gathered and the fact he'd decided not to keep Gamine, I had to wonder if he had been having physical problems for some time. Getting any kind of answers to questions about his health was like pulling teeth and earned me a shrug and an, "I'm fine." I have no idea, other than he just knew and was more than ready.

Just as Callie was my therapy dog after Mom died, JJ stepped up to help me with my dad's death. JJ and I spent some extra time at the house after everyone left following his memorial service. There is just something so final when your second parent dies, and you must start sorting through their belongings in your childhood home. When I think of "home," it still means Whitefish to me, even though I traveled to another state for college and never moved back. I took JJ with me up to "The Mountain" for one last walk around. It was a beautiful autumn day, with the trees turning their brilliant gold color, and the hint of winter in the air. JJ had a blast running around and taking in the smells. For me, it was an incredibly nostalgic goodbye. Big Mountain had been our playground, both during the summers and the winters. It's where my parents met, and my dad bartended with me on his shoulder as a baby. The Chalet, where my mom's office was located, was our childcare and entertainment center. We quickly became ankle-biters on skis, according to the ski patrol, and perfected our jumping skills on courses that wound through the trees, where big skis couldn't navigate. During the summers, we would pick huckleberries with our Saint Bernard, Heidi, who did her very best to make sure she got the lion's share of them. The summer that our house was being built, we lived in the Lodge with said dog, a cat, and two parakeets. Thank goodness, it was long before *The Shining* was released. We were young and not scared about having a large empty place to ourselves. We fed the trout in the pond, laughing as the very over-fed fish jumped to the surface. It was a wonderful adventure from the perspective of my sister and me. Those childhood memories remained clear and happy. JJ and I had hiked up past where the old trout pond had been and under the area where one of the original chairlifts used to be, on which I had made many a trip. Growing up on a ski resort was an idyllic way to spend a childhood. One of my high school jobs was working as a ski instructor. On the days when knee-deep powder had fallen overnight, we could catch the first ride as the chairlifts came to life for the day, putting in the first tracks of the day before it was open to the public. I often got to end my day skiing "sweep" with my dad and the rest of the ski patrol.

A sweep is performed at the end of every day to make sure all the skiers were off the runs, and there was nothing better than getting to ski with my dad. Now, as I sat and looked down at the Chalet, with the familiar view of Whitefish Lake behind it, I knew this last trip up the mountain was the ultimate goodbye. JJ gave me many hugs that day.

Grief is a funny thing that is never as clean-cut as we'd like. Even with time, it doesn't go away, it just changes. Just as we all live our lives differently, people grieve and remember in different ways. I have three of my mom's voicemails saved and periodically listen to them. They don't make me sad. Instead I smile, remembering her strength, even as her voice began to fail her. After Mom died, I loved to call the house and have the answering machine pick up. It gave me the chance to hear my Mom answer in her pre-ALS upbeat voice. Four years later, her voice is imprinted in my memory and gives me a smile when I think about it. When a memory of Mom or Dad brings a tear, JJ knows in an instant that I am sad and she is quick to comfort me. She then usually follows it up with a demand for playtime, done in a way that is sure to make me laugh. We are blessed at home to have this loving, intuitive, and silly dog to share our lives with.

We've talked about it before, but you never know when something will hit you from out of the blue and remind you of your loved ones. It's nostalgic for BossyPants to be close to home around mountains and ski resorts. She about lost it getting coffee in Sandpoint a couple of days ago when looking at the bags of coffee with the names of ski lifts. She was raised on a ski resort in Montana and would go on ski trips to Schweitzer and Fernie with her dad. It will happen when you aren't really expecting it. Just roll with it. And let your dog give you a hug. We help. A lot!

14

Shortly after we opened the Hospice House, I started JJ's Facebook page to feature the stories of her at work and play, as well as sharing other stories of animals that made a difference in people's lives. Originally, the page was designed for friends, family, and the family members of former patients who had expressed a connection to JJ during their time visiting our facility. I decided to set it up in JJ's voice to highlight her personality and her antics. She often has been the one bright spot during a very sad time, and JJ's page was meant as a more lighthearted form of continued bereavement support for those who wanted to follow it. As one visitor said, "Distractions and permission to smile or even laugh is such a good thing at times of impending loss and sadness." It is very touching to have a family member of a patient occasionally comment on a photo and recount a story from their visit that they could smile about. When I get to hear from family members about what a difference JJ has made in their lives, I am deeply honored. As another visitor said: "I am so glad my dad got to interact with JJ before he passed. He used to have a Golden that he adored. So, when he saw JJ it was love at first sight. She was, and is, a furry blessing." At times, JJ's interactions seem very brief, but she is known to visit people often when she knows she is needed. It goes to show just how comforting even a brief visit from a dog can be and it has been fun to be able to continue this virtually on social media.

After the viral video madness happened, I was a bit overwhelmed at first by having so many followers. In the midst of interviews and trying to work, I had constant messages and comments on JJ's page. Jumping from 1385 followers to 65,000 almost overnight is pretty crazy. I had countless requests from across the world asking if I could bring JJ to visit an ailing relative. There were so many questions and messages from people wanting to know how to get started with a therapy dog, I had to scramble to post information about this, and I was never so happy to be proficient with copying and pasting skills. There were many late nights in the first month just trying to keep up with the many messages. While I posted and answered people, JJ took it all in stride with long naps.

After the first month or so, things settled down to a dull roar and I could get back to a normal routine. JJ and I continued to balance out our work schedule with play time at home as well as the obligatory naps, hers much more frequent than mine.

Along the way, I developed a set of core values for JJ's Facebook page once she became so popular. I decided that the page would reflect respect, kindness, and inclusivity, while offering support and education. Most of the new followers were gracious and well mannered and appreciated the same in return. Since end of life care is my passion, and because of JJ's popularity, I now had a way to share with many others the work we do with our hospice patients and families. JJ became an accepted conduit for sharing sensitive and often sad information related to end of life issues. Just as her presence at the Hospice House makes some of the dying process a little bit easier, I have found people more willing to "dip their toes" in the discussion of end of life matters when it is presented through JJ. As one Facebook page follower said, "Thank you for all you teach us by sharing the intimate experience of end of life care. All of you amaze me, and personally, following you and your group has helped me heal after caregiving for my mother, sister, and my fur baby, all whom have passed on in the past four years. I am forever grateful."

My goal is to normalize the dying process as much as I can since none of us get out of it. We see so much added angst at the time of someone's dying simply because family and friends were so deeply uncomfortable with mortality that they avoided talking about the pending death. Bring up the topic in public and watch people flee as if a tornado warning just went off.

As a hospice worker, one of my biggest responsibilities is teaching and preparing patients and loved ones for the changes that will occur as someone's disease progresses. It is a blessing to have the occasional opportunity, such as JJ's page, to get people outside of the Hospice House thinking about what they would want at the end of their life because of the connection to my therapy dog. I work deliberately to balance out the sad and heart-wrenching things with silly, playful, and fun times. Even in our Hospice House, we all experience a wide variety of emotions and that is perfectly normal. The feedback I get on Facebook tells me that I am doing something right. One follower wrote: "Thank you so much for sharing this journey with us. It's helpful for those making end of life decisions, both two-legged and four-legged. As a nurse, I am so glad to see the frank discussion about matters that so many don't want to discuss." And another: "Following JJ helped me with my father's journey with cancer and I understood the true meaning of hospice care."

While many ask me how I can possibly keep up JJ's social media sites, it is truly a labor of love. It has become a natural extension of the work I do as a nurse and taking a few minutes throughout the day has its rewards. The responses from page followers is astounding. "JJ is chicken soup for the soul. She brings joy to everyone she meets. I can't miss a day of her posts to find out what she is up to." Another commented, "Do you ever marvel at how this beautiful girl has brought this internet community together?"

One of the most common comments of concern about the video addressed families abandoning a loved one. Many did not understand the elderly woman in the video simply did not have anyone alive or near to care for her. If you haven't been through the often drawn out dying process with a loved one, it is hard to imagine what it is like. JJ's page has given me the opportunity to explain to others what end of life entails and how it is different for each person and family.

Imagine being with someone in the hospital for a week or two, and the decision is made to change to comfort care, which means aggressive treatment measures are stopped and the focus becomes keeping the person comfortable. At our hospice facility, we always hope that those patients will transfer to us, as it is our specialty to care for those who are actively dying, making sure all symptoms are controlled and assisting loved ones through the process. Hospitals have plenty of caring staff, but they are more focused on the treating of problems rather than guiding people through their last journey. When someone does transfer to us, it can be for hours, days, or another couple of weeks. Not everyone who comes to us dies at the Hospice

House, but a large percentage does. We have families who stay and room in, although we often will encourage people to take breaks to take care of themselves. I don't call myself a Registered Nag (RN) for nothing. Some people simply cannot sit hour after hour keeping vigil at the bedside. Some need to work because they have a family to support and have no paid time off, and some patients have relatives trying desperately to make it from out of the area in time to say goodbye. Others have family members who haven't exactly been told straight up by providers in the hospital how close to death their loved one is, so they feel there is a lot more time despite what we tell them. Those of us in hospice know some patients will wait until all their people leave to go home to take that last breath, which is why we explain to family and friends that it is important that they periodically leave the room, especially if a patient has clearly been lingering a long time with family staying intently at the bedside. Conversely, we have those who appear very close to death but who wait for an important date or person to arrive before letting go. When able, JJ and I will spend some time with those people at the bedside so they are not alone. These moments, coupled with the stories of our Walkouts, are heart-wrenching for many to read and discuss. I am told that posts like this evoke a strong response, but I believe it is essential to shed light on this natural experience. One person summarized exactly my goal in sharing as much as I do through JJ. "I believe one person can make a huge impact. Maybe, TBO, all of these postings might just create a new level of desire in how we recognize and work with people at that point in their life." And hopefully this happens because of JJ. As another commenter wrote: "Just so you know JJ, you and your humans, and cat-dog have brought me a form of therapy by following your page! I went through a very unexpected job change and had a hard time adjusting, and following your page was therapy for me! Keep up your good work."

Yesterday was the case of family being told the prognosis was a week according to the hospital doctor. While The Bossy One always tells people her crystal ball is broken, we have a really good idea here. This gentleman came to us the night before, and while he wasn't responding a whole lot, he did spend time interacting and petting me with a big smile. He had a dog he loved very much at home. Yesterday morning it was clear it was fast approaching the time for him to say goodbye to all of us. We had free time, so after calling his family, we sat with him for his last twenty minutes with me up on the bed for a while and then sitting in TBO's lap for a while nudging his hand every now and again. It was a very peaceful goodbye. His family, while having difficulty understanding how quickly it went, they were thankful to hear how those last minutes went.

While I will post articles on topics such as grieving, whether for people or animals, hospice, empathy, and end of life care, I don't do it every day. These posts often get good discussions going and are shared widely, but can elicit great emotional response as well. It is common to get responses from someone who is touched by what I have shared that day. "Thank you so much for sharing this! Our family is about to experience the loss of a young father of five. What incredible divine timing for this article." Just as life review is done with hospice patients and families, stories and photos are often shared on JJ's page as a way of reflecting on people's own experiences. When I share a photo, story, or article, it often draws out memories. Our own stories give meaning to our lives. People usually like to share and be acknowledged for what they have gone through, whether we are talking about a death in their family or a pet that gives them or others therapy. One person told me how the posts made dying a lot less scary for her after experiencing a sudden loss of several classmates.

Along the way, I make sure to post JJ being silly or having fun, whether at work or at home. Besides the joke of her never-ending quest for more bacon, people get to see her chasing a toy down the hall, retrieving in the most non-retriever-like form, gopher hunting, or having an absolute blast swimming and leaping into the water. Since we spend much more of our time away from work, people delight in watching her antics with the rest of the animals we have. Laughter can be some of the best medicine around for those dealing with any sort of difficult times, and the positive responses JJ gets is beautiful. "Following JJ and her scribe, Tracy, has brought me much laughter and tears. Your patients are so lucky to have such caring caregivers. And we are so lucky you share the journey. For me personally, you have lessened the fear of dying and helped me realize it is the circle of life."

I enjoy keep the page going, and I appreciate the response of everyone who follows. I didn't know how far it could go, though. In the autumn after so many had joined JJ's page, one of her followers suggested that I enter her in a contest after seeing photos of her chariot, our Subaru Outback. It was called the Subaru Pet Hall of Fame contest, and it turned out to have over 7,000 entrants. I decided to enter about halfway through the contest and submitted a photo collage along with a brief story (number of words allowed were limited).

"JJ is a five-year-old Golden Retriever female who is a Therapy, Hospice, and Crisis Response dog. She's prone to sassiness and constantly in search of bacon, while often confused with a male Irish Setter of unknown origin. She works three days each week at an inpatient hospice facility, providing comfort to patients, families, staff, and volunteers. Death and dying is a hard topic for people (I've been a hospice nurse for twenty-two years) and we've found stories about how animals can be a more non-threatening bridge to the conversation that everyone will eventually need to face. We balance heart-wrenching stories with more lighthearted moments on her Facebook page in a way to reach out and support not only families we have served in hospice, but the general public. She also is a Crisis Response K9, responding to national and local crises offering support and comfort. During time off, she explores the country. Our Subaru Outback gets her everywhere she needs to go in style, whether it's work or play."

Entries were voted for online and the top vote-getters were judged by a panel to determine the Grand Prize Winner. It's because of the many people who voted for JJ daily during this contest that she was ultimately judged the winner. I really didn't know what this entailed, but I found out soon enough.

The prize was a trip to Los Angeles, where a video about JJ would be aired during the World Dog Awards. Tellus was not able to go on the trip due to another commitment he had, so I asked my friend Amy to go along. Amy is the Mom of JJ's firedog boyfriend, Casey. We're not exactly LA types, but figured it would be a fun adventure and JJ, of course, would be going along for the ride.

The first step was the making of the video about JJ and the Subaru she rides in. I did my best to deep clean my car so it would be presentable for filming, hoping the "Crazy Dog Lady" decal on my back window would escape notice. A film crew flew into Portland in December during a time when we were experiencing flooding in the Willamette Valley. Luckily, we had arranged to do the outdoor filming at a friend's retriever training property that had several ponds. Many locations were inaccessible that day due to water over the roadways, but this property had many high areas, including the entrance. The weather gods shined upon us that morning, and we could see glimmers of the elusive, winter blue sky. I was nervous in front of the camera, so I had to keep repeating what the producer wanted to get from me. JJ couldn't care less, as she started the first few hours of the day playing and swimming. She got to jump into the water over and over chasing a bumper for the camera and was in her element, despite the very cold water.

The producer knew about JJ's unique "retrieving" form and wanted to get some video of it. We walked over to our friend's back lawn, as it made a nice green backdrop. As I was getting ready to throw the bumper, I heard a "gobble" over my shoulder. I knew by her alert stance that JJ did as well. All I could think of was "no, no, no," as she eyed the young turkey on the deck and headed toward it. The fine art of recall, "NO, HERE," was completely lost on her by that point, as she channeled her inner bird dog. The turkey, seeing her coming, was doing his best to escape through the closed sliding glass door. I had horrified visions of having to call the owners of the house, who were in California, to explain the mayhem of a broken door and the wrangling of a turkey from within the house. Finally, JJ flushed the turkey up onto the porch railing, and as she sailed around for a better vantage point, the turkey flew and took refuge in a very large tree next to the house.

The short clip that made the video had JJ chasing the turkey as it flew with me yelling in the background "JJ, NO!"

Since it was a Subaru award, they wanted to get some shots of me driving my car with JJ sitting in it. What followed was a slow trip through the country roads, with me following an SUV that had its rear door open with the cameraman almost hanging out of it. I needed to be within a couple of feet of the bumper in front of me, and I'm sure my eyes were huge as I drove, terrified I would rear-end them or that the cameraman would accidentally drop something out of their vehicle. It was definitely a "do not do this at home" experience. JJ just hung out in the back seat, but was confused about why I kept trying to get her to sit up, not understanding my pleas of "cooperate for the camera so we can get this done and there will be a ration of bacon in it for you."

After finishing the outdoor portion, we moved to the Hospice House for indoor filming, fortunately just as the rains returned. We spent many more hours interacting with patients and family members, as well as trying to get me to answer questions without tripping over the answers, stammering, or saying "uh." By the end, I couldn't get my brain cells to cooperate, although everyone was very nice and kept telling me I was doing great. I have no idea how actors do their jobs. Ten hours or so of recorded footage was condensed into a one-minute video, ready to be shown on television during the World Dog Awards show.

The trip to Los Angeles was quite an adventure. Since our trip was arranged separately from those who were entrants in the different categories for the awards show, I knew that JJ would not be flying in the cabin with us. This was a purely recreational trip, and I would never try to pass her off as a service dog to get her to fly in the cabin, even though I would have preferred it. She flew in the baggage area in a crate, and Amy and I could watch her load. Fortunately, dogs are last on and first off with Alaska Air. Many of JJ's followers were upset at the thought of her not being in the cabin with me, but we simply were not going to abuse the system, even though so many others do on a regular basis with fake service dogs. I knew when we picked her up that she hadn't been stressed. Her blanket had absolutely no holes in it. If she gets upset, she goes on a tear ripping up her blankets. She came out of her crate, gave herself a good shake and looked at us as if saying "What now?" Later we found out that one of the airlines allowed all the dogs traveling to the awards show to fly in cabin. Oh, well.

All the dogs were staying at one hotel in Beverly Hills, and, as we found out when we arrived, one of the entrants was a pig, who later won the "Most Dog-Like Animal" category. We all had to attend a rehearsal the night before the broadcast. JJ even had her very own publicist assigned to her, Michael. Michael was a great guy, and we all chuckled at this unique assignment, as we wound our way through a myriad of animals. All the entrants seemed to know about all of the other dogs, but somehow we had missed out on all of this. Luckily, we had our phones and could quickly do a Google search during the rehearsal.

Here we are seated on the couch next to a small dog and a miniature horse. And there was a pig too. My people knew it was around by the way I started sniffing the air! Of course, TBO thought it all made for great training opportunities.

The next morning, we wanted to check out Rodeo Drive, so Amy, JJ, and I decided to walk there. We made the mistake of using the phone navigator, which apparently was having an off day or decided we all needed some serious exercise, because it took us on a most interesting route that added six extra miles. Along the way, we were verbally accosted by a man who was highly offended when I would not let JJ greet his dog. We got to play tourist once we finally arrived at our destination, so that was entertaining. But we just shook our heads when we discovered our hotel was really about one and a half miles away. By the time we got back, even my FitBit was worn out. When we shared our adventures with people at the event, they looked at us incredulously. JJ's publicist said, "People don't *walk* to Rodeo Drive."

That night when we arrived at the World Dog Awards, I discovered we were going to walk the green carpet, a nod to the typical red carpet, but in keeping with the theme of the dogs being honored. It was quite something, and I was well out of my element—give me dying patients to take care of any day over dressing in heels for a gala. Luckily, since we were the unknowns, we didn't have a lot of attention placed on us and could make it quickly into the "green" room. It was decked out with an assortment of dog biscuits, along with food for people. As the room filled up with celebrities and dogs, we ended up sitting close to the owners of a Jack Russell Terrier and a miniature horse, whom we were seated next to at the awards show. Since JJ's video hadn't been shown yet, no one knew who we were. Before the show began, we were surrounded by several Subaru executives who wanted to meet JJ, and I overheard an entrant say, "You obviously are someone!"

Amy and I both have specialized training with our Animal-Assisted Crisis Response work—which emphasizes keeping all dogs at safe distances from one another—so we bit our tongues as we watched some close calls between dogs getting into each other's space. The World Dog Award show ran over two hours. I was so relieved to find out that I did not have to walk across the stage when the video was shown.

You all helped me be selected the Subaru Pet Hall of Fame winner. This was something separate from the different categories of the World Dog Awards. We were there to be recognized and have a short video aired about me. We didn't have to walk on stage until the very end, but did have to walk the Green Carpet. I was proud that BossyPants didn't trip and embarrass me. Thank you to everyone who voted for me. It was an honor to have my story told.

Throughout our time at this Subaru-sponsored weekend, JJ went into therapy dog mode randomly, handing out hugs to those she thought needed them. We had frequent interactions with people in the hotel lobby, as guests and staff were eager to enjoy time with her. One of the highlights was when we had the honor of meeting active duty Blackhawk helicopter pilot Brandon Harbaugh, who has served in the Army for fifteen years. He was reunited during the show with his dog Saint, who was given the Award of Loyalty. We also met Brandon's young son, who enjoyed meeting JJ and getting a hug from her. He turned to his dad with a big smile, and said: "She really does make me feel better!"

We spent our last day wandering along Venice Beach, covering over seven miles. It's an area filled with some very interesting characters. JJ would have preferred her beach time be off leash so she could chase the seagulls, though I was glad she was on one since her skateboard-phobia came back to haunt her with so many people on skateboards everywhere along the way. The treat bag got heavy use as we turned it into a training weekend full of many kinds of new experiences. She even got an alligator and sweet potato treat from a colorfully dressed psychic on the boardwalk. But it was a tremendous amount of stimulation, and we were all happy to get back home.

While I didn't set out to have JJ become an international virtual therapy dog, along the way, that is exactly what has happened. I have had messages from fellow hospice workers, nurses, and other medical staff, mental health workers, and people from all other walks of life who routinely follow and check in to see what JJ is doing. I get to hear from those whom we have met for HOPE AACR callouts as well as family members who check in periodically. Her antics help to lighten people's days. It starts with her, but it goes beyond to the support people show each other.

Because the nature of JJ's page and the frank discussions around death and dying that occur, there have been many people who shared their stories just as openly. JJ's Facebook page has become its own community, with some very supportive people following along. Someone can share about their struggles or loss, while getting support and encouragement from others. I am thankful for the people who do share their stories with everyone. It reinforces the positivity and support that other people need.

Even sharing the journey of whelping and raising puppies has developed into a supportive, positive online network. I had no idea how helpful sharing the journey of raising our puppies would be for so many. Distraction, even for a short moment, is good for those who are having difficulties in their lives. I received countless messages of thanks from those who relied on videos or photos of the puppies to get them through the day. Many people describe picking their own favorite virtual puppy to follow along over the eight weeks.

When sad, stressed, or just down, music can be a wonderful mood lift. Be happy today and dance, even if it's just for a moment.

As a long-time follower pointed out, "What a true blessing this page has been for me for such a long time. Generated and driven by love and compassion, whether sharing work, play, grief, Littles, or important family time as well as education. It is just a beautiful space to come to. Thank you." It truly has been a gift to be able to share so much with the public. I don't always get to hear how JJ has made a difference, so when I do, I treasure it. Sometimes, family members of former patients stumble on JJ's page long after they have been at the Hospice House. One visitor wrote, "I love seeing JJ and knowing she is still working at Evergreen in Albany. She was so comforting when my niece and I were there with my brother, and her daddy. JJ comforted all three of us and got my brother's hand on her head where he could give her 'pets' as he called petting a cat or dog. They were bare touches but he knew she was there. JJ came to my niece and me in the hallway, and she knew the overwhelming fear of how close our loved one was to leaving this world. I sat on the floor in the hallway and JJ drew close and showed me her tummy to pet. JJ approached my niece when she came from the room and she sat on the floor with JJ. JJ got close and placed her paw on my niece's shoulder to comfort her. She is a beautiful soul covered in fur with four legs, but in reality, she is an angel in disguise. Thank you, JJ, for being with us the last three days of my brother's life."

One of my most treasured thank you messages comes from someone we've never met, a fellow hospice nurse. He had sent me a photo of his wife looking through JJ's photos on her calendar shortly before she went onto hospice. I was honored to get a card from him after his wife's death. "You both made a difference in our lives these past months, even from so far away, and without us actually meeting. This is important work, and we only have one chance to get it right. Thanks for what you do. Good memories, no regrets." This, on a card with a beautiful drawing of his wife that was illustrated by her daughter and accompanied by the words: "The happy heart is true" on the inside. It was a privilege to be considered a tiny part of her care team, even from so far away. This. This is why I share so much through JJ, whether in person or from afar. It has been a humbling experience and I will forever be grateful for the things JJ has taught me and helped me share along the way.

Those of us who have done hospice work a long time are familiar with the term "visioning." It is now referred to as end of life visions or dreams. Over the years, especially while doing inpatient hospice work, I have been witness to many of these instances. It is a common occurrence at end of life and will get my attention faster than any change in vital signs or even physical changes. It is not the same as drug-induced hallucinations or delirium, as many medical providers and family members think. Most of the time, the person who is dying sees loved ones who have previously died, although I have had people report seeing children and angels. These visions are almost always positive and comforting to the person dying, and to those around them when we explain what is happening. I have told families time and time again that I was always very curious to be able to see what they are seeing. However, that would mean my time would be ending soon, and I'm in no hurry to get to that point.

I know that one day, it will be my turn to face the end of my life. As we take care of those in the midst of dying, my colleagues and I have shared with each other what we think will be most important to us when it is our time. It leaves my husband shaking his head at the way my co-workers and I are all so matter of fact about the details of death, especially our own. While we have had patients who have chosen to be as alert as they possibly can, knowing they will have pain or discomfort if they forego potent medicines, the general consensus among our staff is comfort first. "Give me the good stuff. Do not let me suffer." My own personal priority is "Flip the pillow to the cool side every couple of hours and do not let my lips dry out." Do this work long enough, and indeed it becomes a normal part of life.

Odds are that JJ will die before I do, as our dogs have such a shorter lifespan than we have, but oh, what years we have had, and we are far from done enjoying them. I have no doubt that when it's my turn to die, I will have family, including my parents, who come to see me in my end of life vision. Front and center will be my heart dogs, JJ and Callie, patiently waiting for me to reunite with them and go on that long walk. Dash, Mama Gamine, Taz, Ottie, Goldie, Shylah, Dillon, Lily, Pinch, Heidi, along with Max and his posse of black Labs will be waiting as well. Most likely there will be more; ones I have yet to have the pleasure of meeting.

Until then, JJ and I will continue to work and play, as we have been, until she tells me it's time for her to retire. When that time comes, it will be hard on us all, but she will have earned some fabulous retirement years.

No swimming in the pond today, we got called in to work. This time of year is especially poignant for those who must say their goodbyes to those they love and cherish. Live graciously, love fully, and enjoy the moments you have.

Epilogue

In a short period of time, since originally writing these stories, so many things have changed in our lives. In hospice, we are used to talking about end of life and preparing for goodbyes. However, our hospice staff was not prepared for the weekend Syd, our therapy cat, disappeared. It was well known that he would jump into people's cars and would greet visitors enthusiastically. Over the years, we would hear people periodically mention how he needed to be "rescued" and find a "real home." We would all point out how the Hospice House was his selected home and he was most comfortable wandering when he wanted to, though he did not roam farther than the parking lot and field next to the Hospice House. He had a cozy, heated house at the front door, along with a reliable source of food. One Sunday, several of us started asking one another if we had seen Syd the day before. JJ and I walked the field, looking for him, and we called Animal Control, as well as all the area veterinarians in our search for him. The following Monday, our supervisors even combed through hours of footage from our surveillance cameras trying to determine if someone had taken him. It was a fruitless search, and he simply appeared to have vanished. Over the next several months, we had countless black cat sightings reported. Several of us would check these out, but sadly Syd never came home to us. It's hard to be left without any answers and we miss his presence. There is talk periodically about getting another cat, but I'm not sure how it would work. Syd had such a special connection to others and he was the one who picked us, after all. Thank you, Syd. You were an amazing gift to us all.

Marfa was the first therapy dog used at Evergreen Hospice and the partner of one of our home hospice nurses, Anne. The difficult reality is our animals don't live as long as we do. Marfa was thirteen and a half when she started slowing down significantly. She continued to work, although at a slower pace, until she died in June of 2016. Anne now has a new partner, Chaco, who is learning the ropes and following in Marfa's footsteps.

I have always known that I wanted to have more than one or two dogs that can make therapy visits. This would allow me to rotate them to share in the workload. Shylah will be one to help fill in, but I also knew since JJ was getting older, I needed another prospect. I have always envisioned JJ living a long, grand life, just as her mother has, but want to make sure I don't burn her out. At fourteen-and-a-half, Gamine still is amazingly spry and in relatively good health. She continues to love each day she meets and smiles broadly at any person she encounters. She is slowing down though, and no longer makes therapy visits as her stamina is much less than it was even a year ago. She is the equivalent of ninety-one in people years, and I could only be blessed to have the spunk and good attitude she has when I reach that age.

We decided to keep another puppy to be trained as one of my therapy dogs. We named her Bria, meaning strong and noble, a similar name to Shylah's. Bria is one of JJ's nieces, whom JJ helped raise. I am hopeful Bria will enjoy the work her aunt and nanny so clearly loves, both as a potential therapy dog and HOPE AACR canine partner. At the time of our decision to keep Bria, I knew I would be in no rush with her training, as JJ was only six years old and had plenty of time ahead of her in her therapy dog role. Over the years as a therapy dog handler, I have learned to appreciate the puppy months, as they seem to go by far too quickly. I planned to make Project Canine puppy visits until Bria was 6 months old, just as I had with Shylah. After that, I would continue her training at a pace we were both comfortable with.

In December, one week after Bria's littermates went to their new homes, JJ was due for her annual physical. She had seemed to have just a bit less energy and had excessive thirst for the two days prior to visiting the vet. Because of this, we did a bloodwork panel, but otherwise she checked out just fine. She had been very involved with playing with the puppies whenever she possibly could, so we figured she just needed to catch up on some rest. A few days later, JJ wasn't as interested in food as she normally was, was more tired, and she continued to be very thirsty. When I followed up with the results of the blood work, we discovered her calcium level was alarmingly high. We were given a referral to a specialty clinic and managed to get in before Christmas. While I tried to be optimistic that the cause of her high calcium and corresponding symptoms had a surgical fix due to an endocrine gland gone haywire, I had done my research and I was not surprised when I heard "Lymphoma." Still, my heart sunk to my feet and my stomach was in knots. On the drive home, it struck me how I had been down this exact path before. First with my heart dog, and now with my heart and soul dog. The coincidence of having both Callie and JJ diagnosed with the same cancer, at the same age, in the month of December, while the puppies they were nannies to and mentored waited at home was almost too much to bear. When Callie was diagnosed, JJ had then been the exact same age as a puppy that Bria was now. It made my head spin. I could have done without this uncanny comparison.

While we had chosen not to treat Callie for her cancer, as she had been diagnosed late into her disease, we had other options with JJ. The veterinarians felt we had caught her lymphoma early, as her lymph nodes were only slightly enlarged. Her symptoms were due to the high calcium level caused by the cancer, and the ultimate goal was to try to bring her calcium levels back to the normal range so she would feel better. This most likely would require chemotherapy. When I shared the news about JJ's diagnosis, I had many people ask me how they could help. With the urging of so many wanting to contribute financially to a dog most had never met, I set up a GoFundMe account and met our goal in less than 24 hours. Due to the generosity of so many, we knew we would be able to pursue all necessary diagnostic tests and indicated treatment options. It was incredibly humbling for both Tellus and me, and we are forever grateful.

JJ was immediately started on a steroid called prednisone while we discussed treatment options. We use steroids for symptom management often in hospice patients, so I am very aware of its side effect causing appetite stimulation. Some people can get to the point where they want to eat almost around the clock. Animals are not different, and JJ was in constant search of something to eat. Her charming, mooch behavior went to another level when on prednisone. Luckily, we tapered her off this medication within a few weeks and her ravenous appetite subsided somewhat.

There are different kinds of lymphoma in dogs, as there are in people. As we waited to try to pinpoint if we were facing B-cell or T-cell lymphoma, we discussed the gold-star treatment for this cancer in dogs. It involves a chemotherapy protocol in four-week cycles with three different chemotherapy agents. Typically, treatment runs four cycles and lasts about nineteen weeks if all goes well. As a former chemo nurse, I knew them all. In fact, I used to joke about one of them, Adriamycin, since I had poked my finger when mixing this drug back in the late 1980s. The drug is red-orange in color and requires dilution before giving it intravenously because it can be very hard on tissues if it leaks out of an IV—fortunately my finger was none the worse for wear. The chemo combination for dogs has the same side effects of suppressing the bone marrow's ability to produce white and red blood cells, though it can also cause gastrointestinal side effects such as nausea or diarrhea.

We chose to transfer JJ's care to Oregon State University, where they have a vet school and teaching hospital. They are closer in proximity to us and have access to the latest cancer treatments. When I first called, they were booking new patients almost three months out. Once they reviewed her records—the prognosis of dogs with lymphoma is only one to three months without treatment, so time was of the essence—they found a way to fit her in and we had our first appointment three weeks later. We didn't want to wait to start treatment, so JJ received her first two chemotherapies at the specialty clinic before transferring to OSU.

When vets say dogs in general tolerate chemo well, they aren't kidding. But it's not just because of their canine constitutions; it has to do with how chemo is used. In people, chemo is given in search of a cure, which means higher doses that cause many awful side effects. Honestly, it takes humans to hell and back. But we don't approach pets the same way—we are less willing to put them through such extreme measures that we can't explain to them—and instead of curative measures, we focus on treatments that are palliative in nature. Palliative care focuses on quality of life when choosing treatment options. This means animals are given a less-concentrated amount of chemo with the goal of slowing down or stoping the cancer without making them miserable. From my first discussion with our oncologist at OSU I was reassured that she had this same approach, and I knew we were buying time from the beginning, though as in hospice work, there is no crystal ball.

JJ has been very sensitive to one of the chemo drugs, which often causes her neutrophils, one of her white blood cells, to drop drastically. Our neutrophils are one of the elements that help ward off infection. In people, we have a drug that helps to stimulate production of the neutrophils for cancer patients who need it during treatment, but it is not used in veterinary medicine. Instead, the protocol is to skip a week of chemotherapy to give JJ's bone marrow a chance to bounce back. When her counts are low, she doesn't feel bad at all, but she is at risk for an opportunistic infection. During these times, she is on antibiotics and we cannot go anywhere that might have a high number of dogs. She is cleared to go to work, even when neutropenic, as there are very few zoonotic diseases (disease that can be passed from people to animals) for her to encounter. Otherwise, JJ continues to have high energy, eats well, and feels good. She only has a two to three-day time frame once every month or so when she has no appetite and can have diarrhea. As with people, anticipated side effects can be managed by giving medications ahead of time, which has worked very well for her so far. I'm not sure people fully understood how well JJ has tolerated chemo until we had to have her scheduled at OSU on a workday. I took my lunch break and picked her up in the afternoon and she came back to work with me. She didn't miss a beat, as she passed out hugs, mooched from anyone she could, and ran around happily. On the days we return home from OSU, she immediately runs and plays hard before taking a nap. While people usually lose their hair on the protocol JJ is on, it is much less typical to have alopecia with dogs. However, Goldens do shed their undercoat typically twice a year, and since JJ did this in March, her coat has remained sparse due to the effects of the chemo.

At OSU, she has quickly become a favorite patient, passing out hugs and love to everyone she meets. I was told recently that she spends a lot of time in clinicians' laps throughout the day. One of the techs knew JJ from the Hospice House when we took care of her mother. It is common to read on JJ's discharge paperwork things like "She is such a sweet girl" and "She's the best."

It wasn't until just recently, after three cycles, that she finally seemed to respond to the chemo. Up until this time, she was considered to have partial clinical remission, as her calcium level was staying within normal range and her lymph nodes had not increased in size, but had not decreased either. After her third dose of doxorubicin (Adriamycin), she finally has shown a significant decrease in the size of her lymph nodes. While the oncologists feel this is the medication that JJ's cancer is responding to, it is limited on how many times it can be used. This is due to cardiac toxicity—JJ has now developed a minor heart murmur. As with any treatment, there are pros and cons, and it all must be balanced out in her best interest. Only time will tell how this all plays out, but my husband and I are charged with making the best decisions for JJ, within the perspective of the big picture. This is the essence of good palliative care.

When I wrote in the last chapter about JJ's retirement, I had in my mind "maybe when she's ten or so." The possibility of her mother Gamine outliving JJ seems unfathomable, but here we are. Each week, I drop JJ off for her blood work and chemo treatment, signing paperwork indicating her "DNR" status (Do Not Resuscitate) if something was to happen. While we as people focus on CPR as a good thing to be trained in, only 15 to 30% (depending on which study is cited) of humans survive CPR. In animals, it is an even direr statistic, with less than 10% of pets surviving CPR. I'm sure signing initials next to the code status is very difficult for many pet owners in this situation, but I am again blessed to have my hospice perspective to keep me focused. Now is not the time to waver on end of life decisions. If anything, going through this with JJ has reinforced this philosophy. After going to vet clinics weekly for six months, JJ is no longer happy to walk into a vet hospital and she is clearly stressed while we wait, although I can usually distract her with treats. When we are at OSU, her stress resolves quickly once she is back with the staff, but the experience has made me think of all aspects of her end of life planning. For example, when it is time to let her go, we will not go to a clinic or hospital to do so, unless she is already there. I will have a vet come to the house, ensuring JJ has no stress at the end. Just as I want to have my pillow flipped to the cool side when I am dying, this girl will be in my lap, surrounded by those who love her. Until then, we play, work, eat, and enjoy our days. She is the perfect reminder to live each day to the fullest and she will continue to teach us all to the end.

Appendix

What is the difference between therapy and service dogs?

There is much confusion about the differences. Service dogs and therapy dogs do different jobs, and their training and focus differ greatly as well. A service dog is trained to assist one person with a task or tasks for their specific disability. This role is federally protected under the Americans with Disabilities Act. Therapy dogs make visits out in public and interact with many different people. They are designated as pets and have no legal rights under state and federal laws. Unfortunately, there have been many people who have tried to pass off their dogs as service dogs to obtain access to places pets are not allowed. Most of the time, these dogs behave poorly and are clearly not trained. Fake service dogs are creating problems in the public for those people who have real service dogs. There also is a third designation, Emotional Support Animals, whose main function is to provide emotional support to their handler. These animals are not covered by the ADA laws, but can live in any housing with their handler under the Fair Housing Act.

I would like my dog to become a therapy dog. Where do I get started?

A basic obedience class is a good place to begin this journey. For those interested, the American Kennel Club's Canine Good Citizen (CGC) is a good starting point, and it rewards responsible owners of well-mannered dogs. Many of the obedience components of therapy dog testing are covered in the CGC test as well. Dogs must be able to be approached and sit calmly while being petted by a stranger, be able to walk on a loose leash in a crowd, be groomed, and examined by someone they don't know, show he or she can obey the commands for sit, down, stay, and come when called, be able to be calm around the presence of another dog, not be overly reactive to a distraction, and be able to be held for a short time while the owner goes to another area. When starting with a puppy, AKC has an option called the S.T.A.R. Puppy program, which helps get puppies off to a right start with organized training classes. Even if your dog doesn't become a therapy dog, this kind of training will help ensure he or she is a joy to live with. Many trainers across the country also offer therapy dog preparation classes, where the focus is more on handling skills, exposure to different environments and medical equipment—such as walkers and wheelchairs, learning to recognize stress signals in dogs, and desensitization techniques, to name a few. For those who want to continue training and testing with their dogs, AKC also has advanced CGC programs. JJ has passed both the Urban CGC and Advanced CCG and has many fancy initials behind her registered name.

Are there breeds that are not allowed to be a therapy dog?

There is no age or specific breed that is better for this kind of work, although certainly there are higher percentages of some breeds, such as Golden Retrievers and Labs. Instead of being breed specific, the personality traits of each dog are key to determining the fit for therapy work. At Project Canine, we do not discriminate against any specific breed.

How old must my dog be?

Some people start this training early with a puppy, while others get their older dogs involved for the first time. Whether starting with a puppy or an older dog, a good temperament and a desire to interact with people is a must. Gamine was almost nine years old when she first tested. Most therapy dog organizations have a minimum age of one year for testing. Project Canine has a puppy certification, but it is a very rare puppy that can pass the evaluation. It is most helpful for a dog of any age to be well socialized and possess basic obedience skills.

What does socialization mean?

Many people think socialization means having dogs interact with other dogs. While this is one aspect, socialization means so much more.

It involves introducing a puppy or dog to the sights, sounds, and smells of everyday life, and finding ways to include unique and novel experiences along the way. It must be done in a controlled way, ensuring safe and positive interactions. When a puppy or dog has been exposed to a wide variety of people and other animals, they learn how to appropriately interact in social settings. Ideally, it is most effective when done during early puppyhood, before the puppy reaches 16 weeks old.

What is my role as a therapy dog handler?

It is important for a therapy dog handler to have an interest in interacting with people. While the dog is the star of the show, the handler is the "driver" in not only getting to the visit location, but in making sure those who are interested in having a visit get some time with the dog. I learned early on that most people just want to ask questions about my dog or reminisce about a dog they grew up with. I didn't have to do much other than be a friendly face, but I had to be willing to share my dog and learn to engage with a variety of people. As a handler, I also must advocate for my dog and ensure a positive experience for her each time.

Where do therapy dogs visit?

The beauty of volunteering with a dog is the wide variety of settings available for visiting. Teams read with children, go to nursing facilities, schools, hospitals, VA homes, hospices, detention centers, shelters, and even courtrooms. The various venue options give therapy dog teams an opportunity to try something different if one is not a good fit for handler or dog. During therapy dog volunteer visits, JJ seemed much more drawn to children than older adults. Because of this, I substituted Gamine for our memory care visits, and it was a much better pairing for everyone involved.

Where do I find information about therapy dog groups?

There are many therapy dog organizations in the United States. These groups vary across the country, but I advocate being teamed up with an organization that tests the dog and handler, preferably on a regular basis. Some are nationally based, while many others serve a specific regional area. Legitimate therapy dog organizations also provide liability insurance coverage to teams who pass their screening process. Often the terms "certified" and "registered" are used interchangeably when referring to therapy dogs, however, there is a distinction. Certification meets a higher standard and means teams have been trained to a certain level and tested by the organization. They must be regularly evaluated to ensure the team remains appropriate to perform therapy dog visits. Project Canine has a very high standard for professionalism and safety of the teams certified, and have developed a rigorous screening for such. Registration means the team has simply met the minimum requirements of the therapy dog organization.

I passed my therapy dog test. Now what do we do?

Passing a therapy dog test is just the beginning. It takes time and practice for a new therapy dog and/or handler to get familiar and comfortable with making visits. While Project Canine has incorporated mentoring and shadow visits in the certification process, many other programs do not. I have recommended to new handlers to ask an experienced handler to help with a mentoring process. I know this strategy would have been very helpful to me so many years ago when Booker and I registered for the first time and I was left trying to figure out what the heck I was supposed to do. While therapy dog visits often are an hour or less, with any new dog, I find it important to start with ten- or fifteen-minute visits. This is a time to start building confidence in my dog, so I try to ensure I don't overdo it. Often newer therapy dog handlers have a difficult time noticing how quickly their dog tires out when first doing therapy visits. It can be tempting for new volunteers to be so excited about their new adventure that they overcommit to too many or too long of visits. Overdoing early on can lead to burnout for dog, handler, or both.

My dog gives me so much comfort. I want to share that with other people.

While it is very common for dogs to give love and joy to their own people, it is much less typical for the average dog to want to initiate contact with someone they have never met. It is important to have an honest assessment done for any potential therapy dog in this regard. No matter what the age, the goal in Project Canine is to have dogs that truly enjoy being therapy dogs. We don't want dogs doing it just because their people want them to. We don't want them to be compliant because they just want to please their people, nor do we want them to simply tolerate visits because their owner wants to volunteer. If therapy work is not a good fit for a dog, I encourage people to find other activities their dog shows interest in.

Acknowledgments

There never would have been a book had it not been for an, "I have this idea," message from a publisher, Jaime Levine. Even in my wildest imagination, writing a book had never crossed my mind. After a very long phone conversation, Jaime gave me the confidence to indeed put my stories into words. I am forever grateful for her guidance and editing, and to Diversion Books for taking this project on.

As a young nurse, I had many who helped me in my transition from hospital to hospice work. I will never forget the nurses who taught me how to be a midwife at the other end of the life cycle. Thank you to Nancy, Vickie, Sara Jane, Joanne, and Marge. I channel you often.

To all my co-workers at Samaritan Evergreen Hospice, it has been a privilege to work beside you all. We have created an amazing program, with a great team, and I am so very fortunate to be back at the bedside again. I know I would be in excellent hands if I came here in need of care. I also know my teammates would be shaking their heads laughing, as they turned my pillow to the cool side.

Every time someone recounts a story about their time with JJ at the Hospice House or on a HOPE callout, it makes me smile and renews my spirit. I am so thankful for those who were willing to let me share the myriad of stories here. I am also grateful to Grace for helping to show the world the power of the human-animal connection through a simple touch. Her story has helped to continue the conversation around a very difficult topic.

It has been a great adventure to join the Project Canine team, and I have enjoyed working with Amy, Donna, and Judi as we continue to teach and support new therapy dog teams in Washington State and Oregon.

In the four years since we joined HOPE Animal-Assisted Crisis Response, the number of teams in our region and around the nation has grown tremendously. Through sharing stories of the training and volunteer work JJ and I have done, hopefully more people across the country will learn of the availability of these amazing teams during crises and disasters.

As JJ's cancer treatment has progressed, we have been so fortunate to be cared for by the veterinary oncology team at Oregon State University. While we all know ultimately her care is palliative in nature, they have been amazing at making sure her needs are met along the way. During her daylong stays on treatment day, she gets to share some of her well-known, healing hugs and affection with the team. They, in turn, have made sure to be generous with the cookies. Oncology is such a challenging specialty, whether in people or veterinary medicine. I appreciate their dedication to the pets and owners they care for.

I think of my parents and know how thrilled they would be about this book. They would be especially tickled by the memories of one of my assignments from fifth grade, a story my mom reminded me of shortly before she died. We were tasked with writing an essay, although any specific instructional details escape me. When my essay was returned, written on it was something to the effect of "Tracy, I am disappointed in you. One of your parents clearly wrote this for you." While my parents were voracious readers, neither were particularly skilled at writing. They did instill the love of reading in both my sister and me, and there were many times they would catch me after bedtime with a book and a flashlight under the covers. I can imagine laughing with both of my parents about the irony of the "cheating" young student becoming a published author.

Many of these stories would not have been possible without a goofy, fun loving, perpetually starving, and intuitive dog. JJ placed her trust in me at an early age and has always been willing to go along with my silly ideas. Her antics with my husband and deep adoration of him never fail to make me smile. She has been my partner for all my years as a nurse at the Hospice House and I will always carry her heart and her spirit with me, long after she is gone. Dogs embody the concept of living in the moment. Her motto has become "Barke Diem," a dog's take on Carpe Diem, meaning seize the day. With deep appreciation, I thank my heart and soul dog for the ride of a lifetime. She, of course, would prefer bacon.

Tracy Calhoun RN BSN CHPN has been a hospice nurse for twenty-four years. She was a finalist in 2012 for the March of Dimes Nurse of the Year. Tracy is best known as JJ's "scribe" on social media. She is also an instructor and examiner for Project Canine, a therapy dog organization, and an active volunteer with HOPE Animal-Assisted Crisis Response. She lives in Oregon with her husband, Tellus, and a multitude of animals.

Calhoun's The Color Purple THDD RATN CGCA CGCU, better known as JJ, is a seven-year-old Golden Retriever. She is a therapy, hospice, and crisis response dog who is prone to sassiness and constantly in search of bacon. She often is confused with a male Irish Setter of unknown origin, no matter how many flowers she wears on her collars while at work. JJ works three days each week with Tracy at Samaritan Evergreen Hospice House, providing comfort to patients, families, staff, and volunteers. Over the years, JJ has become an international virtual therapy dog, helping others to celebrate the power of the human-animal bond and approach the often-scary topic of end of life, whether it be people or pets. She was voted Subaru's Pet Hall of Fame winner in 2015. In an ironic twist, JJ now has a connection with patients as she never has before. She was diagnosed with lymphoma in December 2016 and has been undergoing treatment. During her days at the veterinary teaching hospital, she continues to give love and hugs to those caring for her, including a radiology tech whose mother was cared for at the Hospice House.